MW01087787

# Christ
## at Work in You

### The Continuing Function
### of the Risen Lord Jesus

James A. Fowler

C.I.Y. PUBLISHING
P.O. BOX 1822
FALLBROOK, CALIFORNIA 92088-1822

# CHRIST AT WORK IN YOU

Copyright ©2005
by James A. Fowler

ISBN 978-1-929541-47-8

Published by

**C.I.Y.** PUBLISHING
P.O. BOX 1822
FALLBROOK, CALIFORNIA 92088-1822

# Acknowledgements

As I began to share the content of these studies with the participants of the Neighborhood Church, it was Mr. Den Larsen who suggested that this could be represented in a dialectic chart. Thank you, Den, for the "spark of insight" that became the organizing outline of this book.

Appreciation must also be expressed to Sylvia Burnett, my sister (both biologically and spiritually). She provided the editing and formatting that makes this book attractive and readable.

My dear wife Gracie endured the many weeks when materials were spread out on the kitchen table as I wrote these pages. Thank you, sweetheart!

James A. Fowler
July 2005

# Contents

# Introduction

The superficiality of our culture has permeated the mind-set of the Western church. The "cheap grace"[1] that Bonhoeffer warned about has fostered an "easy-believism" that has allowed a superficial assent to Christianity that requires no real change or sacrifice.

In a culture that advocates "safe sex," we have similarly developed a "safe" form of Christianized religion wherein no one is responsible for his actions. There is no doubt that God hates this farcical masquerade of role-playing, for it is totally alien to the dynamic reality of the living Lord Jesus manifesting His life in receptive Christian people.

Hundreds of thousands of people have responded to the evangelistic invitations of Billy Graham and other evangelists or preachers. They have joined various churches, attending catechism and new member classes where they learned the basic facts of Christian doctrine. Baptized and confirmed, they became "voting members" involved in their churches. They serve on committees, in leadership positions, and even behind the pulpit, but their faithful, loyal and dedicated

1

"service" is often but a sterile form of "churchianity" that is devoid of the Christ-life that constitutes Christianity.

How can genuine Christians be content with going through the motions of ritualistic religion? How can they be content with cultural accommodation that adapts to the world's ways under the pretext of "relevance" and seeking to "be all things to all people" (I Cor. 9:22)? How can they be content with periodic "highs" of emotional experience that are inspiring, exciting, and "moving"? How can they be content to have their ears tickled with inspirational pabulum and the panacea of peace that proclaims, "All is well"?

Many who call themselves "Christians" seem to be oblivious to and unconcerned about the fact that the character of their behavior is selfishly misrepresentative of Jesus Christ, and fails to manifest the "fruit of the Spirit" (Gal. 5:22,23).

———————  ♥  ———————

*Jesus clearly indicated that a person's spiritual condition would be evidenced by the "fruit" of his behavior (Matt. 7:16-23).*

Since a Christian is a "Christ-one" in whom the Spirit of Christ dwells (Rom. 8:9), if the character of Christ is not being evidenced in a person's life, then it is legitimate to question whether that individual is a Christian despite his profession of such.

It is not possible to be a nominal Christian "in name only," or a depository Christian who claims to have received Christ into his heart but has no evident desire for intimacy with the living Lord Jesus and no apparent growth in character expression. Those who seem to be content with a false hope that they have a ticket to heaven, or a pass to wave at St. Peter when they get to the pearly gates of Paradise, must be confronted with the fact that it is possible to be a professor of Christ who is not a possessor of Christ.

Christian salvation is not a static transaction whereupon one "got saved" at a particular point in time by engaging in prescribed activities. Salvation involves being "made safe" from the dysfunction of satanically abused humanity, in order to function as God intended as the expressive vessel of divine character.

Genuine Christianity must not adapt itself to the games that the world plays with names, labels, and positions. Christianity is the dynamic reality of the living Christ within us functioning as Savior, continuing to save us from the domination of sinful patterns in our lives as He overcomes such by His character.

Christian literature throughout the ages has consistently explained that the superficiality of easy-believism does not constitute genuine Christianity. A.W. Pink cautioned,

> Do you imagine that the Gospel is magnified or God glorified by going to the worldlings and telling them that they may be saved at this moment by simply "accepting Christ" as their Savior, while they are wedded to their idols, and their hearts are still in love

with sin? If I do so, I tell them a lie, pervert the gospel, insult Christ, and turn the grace of God into lasciviousness.[2]

The missionary statesman Norman P. Grubb wrote,

The only infallible, inexorable consequence of a sinner receiving salvation is not always made plain by Gospel preachers. It is often easy to get the impression that it is certainly necessary to have our sins forgiven, to be delivered from the wrath to come, to receive an assured entrance into heaven; but to submit to the total control of Christ is something which may and should follow, but does not necessarily do so; and even that it is possible to enjoy the former without the latter. Nothing could be more false or absurd. There is no salvation conceivable, possible or actual, other than God's way in infinite grace, of destroying the false form of life in which man lives, and replacing it by the true. The false form of life is that which has "self" in the centre; the true form of life is that which has God at its centre – Christ living in me.[3]

Though some who call themselves "Christians" seem to be oblivious to the misrepresentations of their lives, there are others who suspect there is "something more" to the Christian life than they have experienced. In the words of the song made popular by Peggy Lee, they are asking, "Is that all there is?"

Sometimes they meet a Christian person who has a vital and vibrant personal relationship with the living Lord Jesus, and they make comments like: "Jesus seems so real to you. It's as if you believe that Jesus really talks to you, and walks with you, day by day." They ask questions like: "Do you really think that God is personally orchestrating your life? How can you be so sure that Jesus lives in you, and that God is working in your life?"

The Spirit of Christ is often working in these individuals causing them to hunger and thirst for the fullness of what He wants to be and do in their lives.

# 1

## The Work of Christ – Past and Present

Many Christians seem to think that the work of Christ was completed and terminated when Jesus was historically crucified on the cross. If that were true, then Jesus was but another dead martyr to be remembered in history.

From the cross Jesus exclaimed, "It is finished!" (John 19:30). That statement was not a cry of defeat or termination, but a declaration of victory. Jesus was declaring that redemption was accomplished by the remedial action of His death, as He vicariously and substitutionally submitted to the "power of death" (Heb. 2:14) and paid the price (cf. I Cor. 6:20; 7:23) of the death consequences of sin (cf. Gen. 2:17).

Also inherent in His exclamation was the declaration that by His death He was setting in motion the inexorable completion of the full restoration of mankind to the intent for which God had created man.

"It was impossible for Him to be held in death's power" (Acts 2:24), Peter explained, and God raised Him up in resurrection victorious over death. By His resurrection, the One Who is "resurrection and life" (John 11:25) made His risen life available to mankind in regeneration (I Peter 1:3).

The receipt of the life of the risen Lord Jesus in regeneration is not the completion of the work of Christ in the Christian, either. The living Lord Jesus – "made both Lord and Christ" (Acts 2:36), and "declared the Son of God with power by the resurrection from the dead" (Rom. 1:4) – seeks to administer His governance in the lives of Christians by continuing His saving work.

---------- ♥ ----------

*His "saving death" was singularly and totally sufficient for redemption,*
*but by His "saving life" (cf. Rom. 5:10)*
*the risen Lord and Savior continues to save Christians*
*from the patterns of selfishness and sin*
*that residually remain in the desires of their soul.*

The entirety of Christ's work in Christian experience, whether justification, regeneration, sanctification, or glorification, was encompassed in His declaration of the victory of His "finished work."

When the Person and work of Jesus Christ are limited to historical and theological discussions of the incarnated Person of Jesus and His redemptive mission within history, there is a great restriction to the fullness of the gospel. The studies of Christology (the study of the Person of Jesus Christ) and soteriology (the study of the work of Christ in redemption and salvation) are often allowed to constrict the work of Christ by failing to consider the continuing function of the risen Lord and Savior after His crucifixion, resurrection, ascension, and Pentecostal return in Spirit form (cf. II Cor. 3:17,18).

Christianity was not intended to be just an historical society for the remembrance of the historical Jesus. Neither was the Christian community to be simply a theological society for the formulation of accurate explanations of the historical Christ event.

Christianity cannot be properly understood apart from the eternal ongoing dynamic of the life of the risen Lord Jesus continuing His work as Lord and Savior of mankind.

The Truth (cf. John 8:32,36; 14:6) of the Christian gospel must not be entombed in static categories of ideological conceptions. "Salvation," for example, must not be regarded as a static commodity that is dispensed by Jesus as a benefit to those who will assent to His Being.

Salvation is not a static "eternal life package" that is placed "on deposit" within the Christian believer or in a heavenly repository for future enjoyment. Jesus Christ is now and forever the "eternal life" (cf. John 11:25; 14:6; I John 5:12,13) of God, and He functions dynamically in His work as eternal Savior to cause His "saving life" to overcome sin.

In His function as Savior, He does not simply "make us safe" from erroneous spiritual thinking, or "make us safe" from a destiny in hell, but He continues to "make us safe" from the dysfunctional humanity that derives from a spiritual source other than Himself (cf. Eph. 2:2,3; I John 3:8), in order that we might function as God intended by the presence and expression of the divine life and character in human behavior. There is no salvation apart from the dynamic function of the living Savior, Jesus Christ.

## Dialectic Balance

To explain how the living Lord Jesus continues His dynamic function as Savior, this study will be graphically formatted in the form of a dialectic tension (cf. Addendum A).

An explanation of "dialectic" is probably necessitated. A dialectic format considers two concepts or realities and brings them into logical dialogue with one another. The objective is not to cause one to rise above the other and overcome the other, but to allow a "both-and" interaction of the two. They are not meant to compete with one another, but to complete one another. Both premises are required, and like "two sides of a coin," they cannot be separated one from the other. They exist in a co-relational balance whereby the one provides clarifying definition and context to the other, without attempting to overcome or suppress the other.

This balanced tension of two premises is differentiated, therefore, from dualism, which in its classic definition posits two equal powers that are counterbalanced in a stalemate. A paradox posits two opposites that are juxtaposed to note their polarized distinction. An antinomy, meaning "against the law of reason," notes two concepts that form an unreasonable and irresolvable contradiction. Socratic synthesizing regards one premise as the "thesis" and another as the "antithesis," and seeks to bring them together in a unified "synthesis." A dichotomy, etymologically defined as "cut in two," creates a bifurcation of two ideas into an "either-or" polarity.

Whereas dialectic necessitates a "both-and" counterbalance, the failure to preserve such balanced tension by allowing one or the other concept to be pushed to its extreme by overcoming, neglecting or denying the other, allows for the development of an "either-or" dichotomy. These dichotomous extremes are noted in the outer columns of the graphic in the addendum.

Western thought in general, and Western theology in particular, has always had great difficulty with dialectic balance. Steeped, as they are, in Aristotelian logic categories, demanding clear-cut cause and effect syllogisms or synthesized conclusions, Western thinkers usually eschew the counter-tension of dialect, desiring that everything be figured out in logical categories. Western thought wants clearly defined presuppositions that allow for formulas and equations producing a patent result. The resultant systematization of thought creates static boxes of ideology that become settled fixations, wherein the adherents are unwilling to consider alternative ideas.

Dialectic, on the other hand, requires a dynamic interplay of concepts and ideas kept in tensioned balance with due respect for the alternative.

With this dialectic format in mind, we proceed to consider the completed victory that every Christian has in Christ, alongside of the continuing necessity of dealing with sin in the life of every Christian. By faith every Christian participates in "the victory that overcomes the world" (I John 5:4), and is able to "overwhelmingly conquer through Him Who loved us" (Rom. 8:37), because we are all "complete in Christ" (Col. 2:10). At the same time, "If we say we have no sin, we are deceiving ourselves, and the truth is not in us" (I John 1:8), for we all have "sin which so easily entangles us" (Heb. 12:1), and must agree with Paul concerning the "sin that indwells us" (Rom. 7:17,20,21,23).

How do we reconcile these seemingly contradictory concepts without denying one or the other? Can they be maintained in the tensioned balance of dialectic thinking? The objective of this study will be to provide answers to those questions.

# Jesus is Lord and Savior

The risen and living Christ is the eternal Lord and Savior. He cannot cease to be Who He is. He cannot refrain from functioning as Who He is.

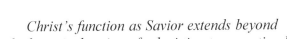

*Christ's function as Savior extends beyond
the historical action of submitting to execution by
crucifixion on the cross of Calvary
for the redemption of the death consequences of sin.*

Christ's function as Lord is more than a theological assertion of deity, sovereignty, or abstract authority. In His Person and work, Jesus Christ always functions as Lord and Savior, and certainly continues to do so as He indwells the Christian.

A strange separation of Christ's Being and function has developed in modern evangelicalism. There are some who advocate that an individual can "accept Jesus as their Savior" to become a Christian, and then later can "accept Jesus as their Lord" to become a disciple of Christ. This dissection of the Being and function of Jesus into two parts became the issue of the "lordship salvation" debate of the late 20th century in American evangelicalism. Unfortunately the debate tended to polarize the two sparring groups, rather than finding the balance of the two truths of the dialectic of Christ's work as Lord and Savior. Christ's function as Lord and

Savior is always conjunctive, and neither can legitimately be separated from the other.

In his book, *I Call It Heresy*, A.W. Tozer wrote:

> To urge men and women to believe in a divided Christ is bad teaching for no one can receive half of Christ. Any message that presents a Savior who is less than Lord of all cannot claim to be the gospel according to Jesus. He is Lord, and those who refuse Him as Lord cannot use Him as Savior.[4]

> The Lord will not save those whom He cannot command. He will not divide His offices. You cannot believe on a half-Christ. We take Him for what He is – the anointed Savior and Lord who is King of kings and Lord of all lords! He would not be Who He is if He saved us and called us and chose us without the understanding that He can also guide and control our lives.[5]

The "Lord and Savior, Jesus Christ" (cf. II Peter 1:11; 3:2,18) always acts in accordance with Who He is in the entirety of His Being. He does not act as a Jekyll and Hyde (Savior and Lord) schizophrenic. The ontological dynamic of His "Being in action" will always combine His Being and function as Lord and Savior.

The ancient Latin scholastics used the phrase, *actio sequitur esse*, indicating, "the action is in accordance with the being that acts." Since Jesus Christ is Lord and Savior, He will always act as such.

Experientially, there may seem to be a sequence of Christ's function, for in accepting by faith His redemptive work as Savior of mankind, an individual enters into a personal relationship with Christ wherein His function as authoritative Lord is accepted with submissive consent.

Accepting Jesus Christ as Savior, however, does not "make Him Lord," for He is eternally the divine Lord. Functioning as the Lord in a Christian's life, He continues to do His saving work of "making us safe" from the residual sin-patterns formed in the desires of our soul. His continued saving function in the Christian does not actuate His function as Lord, rather it is in the context of His Lordship that the living Christ continues to do His saving work of dealing with the sin in our lives.

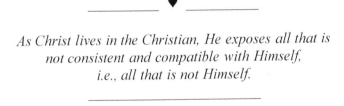

*As Christ lives in the Christian, He exposes all that is not consistent and compatible with Himself, i.e., all that is not Himself.*

The living Lord demands exclusivity. He said in the Sermon on the Mount, "No one can serve two masters, for either he will hate the one and love the other, or he will be devoted to one and despise the other" (Matt. 6:24; Luke 16:18).

As the loving Lord, He jealously desires that the Christian not be a slave of unrighteousness, but a "slave of righteousness" (Rom. 6:16-19), of Himself. The Lord of Righteousness will of necessity find all selfism, selfishness, egoism, and egocentricity to be antithetical to Himself and incompatible with His own Being. As such, it is intolerable, and His holy character will act to "separate" such from His presence in us as He functions in grace to overcome such.

If, as the Holy Lord, He did not deal with all selfishness and sin contrary to Himself, then He would present Himself as an impotent lord, a figurehead lord, a "lord in name only," a Lord that does not act in accordance with Who He is. This cannot be, for God does what He does, because He is Who He is.

The Greek word for "lord" (*kurios*) is the same word that is translated "master" (cf. Matt. 6:24). The word implies ownership, as well as deterministic and functional control. In the ancient world a master owned the slaves and had a right to expect his slaves to submit to his desires with unquestioned obedience. Jesus asked, "Why do you call Me 'Lord, Lord,' and do not do what I say?" (Luke 6:46).

In obedience to Christ as Lord, new covenant Christians are to "listen under" the instructional desires of our Lord, and to be receptive in faith to the grace dynamic of His activity in our lives. We are not our own (I Cor. 6:19,20; 7:23; Rom. 14:7), but we are His to do with as He wills.

Thomas Merton explains,

Every baptized Christian is obliged by his baptismal promises to renounce sin and to give himself completely, without compromise to Christ. As Paul reminds us (I Cor. 6:19), we are "not our own." We belong entirely to Christ. Our thoughts, our actions, our desires, are by rights more His than our own.

Sin is the refusal of spiritual life, the rejection of the inner order and peace that comes from our union with the divine will. It is not only a refusal to "do" this or that; it is more radically a refusal to be what we are, a rejection of our mysterious, contingent, spiritual reality hidden in the very mystery of God. It is a refusal to be what we were created to be – sons of God, images of God.

All of us who have been baptized in Christ and have "put on Christ" as a new identity, are bound to be holy as He is holy. Our actions should bear witness to our union with Him. He should manifest His presence in us and through us.[6]

Watchman Nee referred to the Lord Jesus in the Christian as "the resident boss," but He is more than just an authoritative ruler. Jesus is our life. He is the essential basis of who we are – our spiritual identity as a "Christ-one." He desires to be "all in all" of us, and to express His character in our behavior unto His own glory.

What a tragic misunderstanding some Christians seem to have concerning the Lordship of Jesus Christ. Some have stated, "I am willing to assent to His being Lord, but I just don't want Him to 'lord it over me'!" Some Christians shy away from submitting to Christ as Lord because they consider it to be a loss of personal freedom, a loss of personal rights, a loss of self-control. Indeed it is, but Christ desires to control our lives in such a way as to bring the ultimate freedom of functioning in the context of divine love.

*The final "fruit of the Spirit" mentioned in Galatians 5:23 is not "self-control," as many versions translate the word, but "godly control of the self," whereby we submit to His desires.*

To affirm that "Jesus is Lord" (Rom. 10:9; I Cor. 12:3), the earliest statement of faith among Christians, is to submit to His every desire in our lives. When He is everything to us, and all we want is what He wants, then we have "sanctified Christ as Lord in our lives" (I Peter 3:15) and are allowing Him to function as "our sanctification" (I Cor. 1:30). This sanctification is the continued saving action of the Savior as he "makes us safe" from dysfunctional sin-patterns and sinful misrepresentations of His character.

When the angel directed Joseph to name Mary's son "Jesus," the explanation was, "He will save His people from their sins" (Matt. 1:21). We are His people who are being saved from our sins. Paul explained to the Roman Christians, "Having been reconciled to God, we shall be *saved by His life*" (Rom. 5:10), participating in the ongoing "saving life of Christ."

Serving as the permanent high priest, the living Lord Jesus is "able to *save completely* those who draw near to God through Him, since He always lives to make intercession for them" (Heb. 7:25). The Lord Jesus continues to function as the eternal Savior in the lives of Christians.

# Differentiating Spirit and Soul

To properly understand the work of Jesus within the Christian, as He functions conjunctively as Lord and Savior, requires a differentiation of spirit and soul – of our spiritual condition and psychological behavior. What a disservice theology has done for centuries by attempting to amalgamate spirit and soul as synonymous terms, even to the extent of regarding their differentiation as heretical.

The biblical evidence sufficiently differentiates these differing functionalities of our humanity. Writing to the Thessalonians, Paul indicated that to be "sanctified entirely," our "*spirit* and *soul* and *body* must be preserved complete" (I Thess. 5:23). The writer to the Hebrews notes, "The word of God is living and active and sharper than any two-edged sword, piercing as far as the division of *soul* and *spirit* . . . and able to judge the thoughts and intentions of the heart" (Heb. 4:12).

When we fail to differentiate spiritual function and psychological function, we end up with a mushy merging of psychologized spirituality or spiritualized psychology. Christians are left with an inability to explain the fixed condition of their spiritual union with the Spirit of Christ, alongside of the behavioral conflict in their soul. This is the breeding ground of the false identities, insecurity, and hypocrisy, which are rampant in the contemporary Christian community.

# Our Spiritual Condition

Many Christians have not understood what was brought into being in their spirit by spiritual regeneration. Jesus told Nicodemus, "You must be born again," explaining, "that which is born of the Spirit is spirit" (John 3:5,6). If the life of the risen and living Lord Jesus has not been birthed in our spirit, then we are not Christians. "If any man does not have the Spirit of Christ, he is none of His" (Rom. 8:9), Paul wrote. On the other hand, if we have received the life of the Spirit of Christ, "the Spirit bears witness with our spirit that we are children of God" (Rom. 8:16).

Christians are those who are "born again to a living hope through the resurrection of Jesus Christ from the dead" (I Peter 1:3). They are "alive unto God in Christ Jesus" (Rom. 6:11), with the very resurrection-life of Jesus dwelling in them. A spiritual exchange has been enacted whereby they have been "converted from darkness to light and from the dominion of Satan to God" (Acts 26:18). Previously we "were by nature children of wrath" (Eph. 2:3), but now the Christian has "become a partaker of the divine nature" (II Peter 1:4). This is a radical spiritual exchange, not to be considered as a joint-tenancy of two natures that allows for a dualistic and schizophrenic basis of identity, as well as a paranoid uncertainty of servitude. "No man can serve two masters" (Matt. 6:24), Jesus declared.

Much of the evangelical emphasis on being "born again" has been shallow and misleading. People have been led to think that just because they have raised their hand, walked an aisle, and repeated a creedal statement, they are promised a ticket to heaven with the future guarantee of eternal life. Christianity becomes an "escape hatch" or a "fire insurance policy" to avoid the terrifying threat of hell-fire.

If this is the extent of what it means to be "born again," then it is no wonder that many have accepted the possibility of being spiritually "still-born," with no life expression of growth, maturity, and developing sonship. Such a suggestion of spiritual "still-birth" is not far removed from that of "spiritual abortion" whereby those who are unwilling to go through the labor and pain of Christ being formed in them (Gal. 4:19) participate in the abortion of Christ's life, though they might be adamantly opposed to physical abortion.

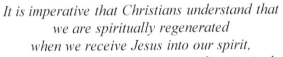

*It is imperative that Christians understand that we are spiritually regenerated when we receive Jesus into our spirit, when His very Being is present and active in the spiritual core of our being.*

"This is the mystery," Paul advised the Colossians, "Christ in you, the hope of glory" (Col. 1:27). He questioned the Corinthians, "Do you not recognize that Jesus Christ is in you – unless you fail the test?" (II Cor. 13:5). "It is no longer I who live," he explained to the Galatians, "but Christ lives in me" (Gal. 2:20).

But even this glorious truth of the indwelling Christ in the Christian can degenerate into mundane statements of the location and placement where Jesus is deposited as a static commodity, failing to understand and appreciate that the living Lord and Savior, Jesus Christ, has become our life (cf. Col. 3:4).

This dynamic of divine life within the Christian disallows spiritual regeneration to be viewed as a static end in itself, and requires that we view regeneration as an initial receipt of the life of Christ, which must be dynamically lived out in our behavior. Regeneration is a crisis with a view to a process.

The spiritual relationship that the Christian has with Jesus Christ as Lord and Savior must not be viewed as a casual acquaintance. In its broadest definition, a "relationship" is merely the locative proximity of two or more objects. The personal relationship of the Christian and Christ, however, is a dynamic relationship that goes beyond placement and proximity to a relational union with Christ.

"The one who joins himself to the Lord is one spirit with Him" (I Cor. 6:17). This is not an essential oneness of equivalence, but a relational union of interactive conjunction, wherein the character of God is allowed expression in human behavior.

Thomas Merton wrote,

Christian holiness is not a mere matter of ethical perfection. Sanctity is not constituted only by good works or even by moral heroism, but first of all by ontological union with God "in Christ." Our ontological holiness is our vital union with the Holy Spirit.[7]

When the Christian is spiritually regenerated – i.e., brought into being again with the life of Jesus in the individual, and that facilitated by the receptivity of faith – a relational spiritual union is established that must allow for the outworking of Christ's life in the Christian's behavior.

Everything becomes new for the Christian. "If any man is in Christ, he is a new creature; the old things passed away; behold, new things have come" (II Cor. 5:17). Whereas once we were identified as an "old man" (Rom. 6:6; Eph. 4:22; Col. 3:9), we have been spiritually transformed into a "new man" (Eph. 4:24; Col. 3:10). The "old man" identity has been crucified (Rom. 6:6), "put off" (Eph. 4:22; Col. 3:9), and eradicated – replaced by the "new man" identity of Christ's presence in our spirit, allowing us to participate in "newness of life" (Rom. 6:4).

The "new heart and new spirit" that Ezekiel prophesied (Ezek. 36:26) has been given to us by the presence of the Spirit of Christ in our spirit. This was not a "heart transplant" or a "parts replacement," but the enlivening of our spirit by Christ's life as the "law of God is written on our hearts" (Heb. 8:10; 10:16).

———— ♥ ————

*The Christian is not just redeemed, a "sinner saved by grace," but the Christian is restored to God's intent for mankind.*

23

We have "all things in Christ" (I Cor. 3:21-23), "all things pertaining to life and godliness" (II Peter 1:3), "every spiritual blessing in heavenly places in Christ Jesus" (Eph. 1:3). We are "complete in Christ" (Col. 2:10).

We need to be aware of our spiritual identity as "sons of God" (Gal. 3:26), "children of God" (John 1:12; I John 3:10), and "saints" (Rom. 8:27: Eph. 1:18; 4:12), who are now "godly" (II Peter 2:9), "righteous" (Eph. 4:24; II Cor. 5:21), and "perfect" (Phil. 3:15; Heb. 12:23).

Every facet of Christ's character is available to us in the "fruit of the Spirit" (Gal. 5:22,23), and the entirety of His functional ministry is made available via the *charismata*, the gifts of the Spirit.

_____ ♥ _____

*Everything that God wants us to have,*
*for everything that He wants to do in us,*
*is accorded to us by the indwelling presence and*
*function of the living Lord Jesus.*

The saving activity of the Savior has been completed in reference to the spiritual condition of every Christian. "For by grace you have been saved through faith" (Eph. 2:8). Spiritually, the Christian has been "made safe" from the dysfunction of satanic misuse and abuse. We are "safe sons," who are "dead to sin, but alive to God in Christ Jesus" (Rom. 6:11), and the Christ Who lives in us and has become the basis of our identity "does not sin" (I John 3:9), allowing for the possibility that we "may not sin" (I John 2:1).

—————— ♥ ——————

*The perfection of our spiritual condition must not, however, obscure the ongoing activity of Christ the Savior in our soul.*

As "new creatures in Christ, all things have become new" (II Cor. 5:17) spiritually, but this is not to deny or disallow that there is a continued renewing (cf. Rom. 12:2; Eph. 4:23) still necessitated in the soul.

Joshua's victory at Jericho still required the people of God to "take the land and overcome the strongholds." In like manner, we who "have been saved" (Eph. 2:8) must still be "saved by His life" (Rom. 5:10). We who are "perfect" (Phil. 3:15) must still be "perfected" (Phil. 1:6; Col. 1:28). We who are spiritually "made righteous" (Rom. 5:19) must "present our members as instruments of righteousness to God" (Rom. 6:13).

Paul explained that the "new man" (Col. 3:10) continues to be renewed as he allows Christ to overcome the old ways of "anger, abusive speech, lying," etc. (Col. 1:8,9).

# 2

## Sinful Patterns in the Soul

The Christian who is a spiritual "new man" still retains old patterns of selfishness and sinfulness in the soul. These action and reaction patterns often present themselves in "old ways" of behavior that are not indicative of the character of Christ.

These old patterns of behavior misrepresent who we are in Christ, but they do not necessarily cause us to revert to being an "old man." The "old man" is the unregenerate person, and while the spiritually regenerated "new man" may misrepresent the character of the One Who is the basis of his identity, he is not in constant danger of apostatizing and becoming an "old man" again.

*Though the Christian is no longer identified as a "sinner" (Rom. 5:19), for his new spiritual identity is that of a "saint" (Eph. 4:12), many residual patterns of sinfulness remain within the soul of a Christian.*

These are the patterns of how we learned to act and react as we dealt with situations and persons during our previous days of sinfulness.

Yes, the Christian is "dead to sin" (Rom. 6:2,11) and no longer a "slave to sin" (Rom. 6:17), meaning that sin, with its personified satanic source (cf. I John 3:8), has no right to reign as master in our lives and hold us under its tyranny. But within the soul, Paul can still write of the "sin that indwells me" (Rom. 7:17,18,20,21,23).

This "indwelling sin" is not a substantive "hunk of evil" within the Christian, nor is it the personified presence of Satan within the Christian, but it is the patterns of sinful action and reaction within the desires of our soul. Ancient Christian writers often referred to the Christian experience of *dipsychia*, the divided soul or psyche, divided by the "desires of the flesh" and the "desires of the Spirit" (Gal. 5:17).

The apostle Paul could refer to Christians as "perfect" (Phil. 3:15), and yet just three verses previously he had confessed that he had not "already become perfect" (Phil. 3:12) behaviorally. The perfecting process, the maturing process, and the growth process of the Christian life is the continuing process of sanctification within the soul of a Christian.

Writing to the Galatians, Paul asked, "Did you receive the Spirit by works of the Law, or by hearing with faith?" The obvious answer is the latter, for only by grace through faith do we receive the Spirit of Christ in regeneration.

Following with another question, Paul asks, "Having begun by the Spirit, are you now being perfected by the flesh?" (Gal. 3:2,3). Again, the obvious answer is to deny that the ongoing process of sanctification and perfection can be effected by any means other than the power of the Spirit of Christ – and certainly not by an alleged "independent self" who falsely thinks it can auto-generate and self-produce divine character by the "works" of self-effort and performance in accord with some behavioral standards of conduct and morality that have been codified into "Christian law."

All Christians are in the process of dealing with their idiosyncratic patterns of sinfulness and selfishness, but the means of overcoming our "indwelling sin" is not by legalistic efforts to conform, but by allowing Christ the Lord to overcome such by His character.

Writing to the Christians in Asia Minor in the latter years of the 1st century, the apostle John noted the necessity of Christians being aware of and admitting to their sinful behavior patterns. He was combating the nascent Gnosticism that advocated an elitism whereby one could be spiritually elevated above all sin.

John replied, "If we (Christians) say (as the developing Gnostics say) that we have no sin (tendencies, propensities, or expression), then we are deceiving ourselves, and the Truth (Jesus Christ – cf. John 14:6) is not in us" (I John 1:8). But "if we confess (Greek *homologeo* – agree and concur with God that our sin is contrary to His character) our sins, then He is faithful and just to forgive us our sins (applying the forgiveness that resulted from the redemptive sacrifice of Jesus Christ), and to cleanse us from all unrighteousness (by the cathartic overcoming of Christ's character)" (I John 1:9).

Thomas Merton declared,

> The Christian faith is "extreme." Once it has "found" Christ, it sees the obligation to break completely with everything that is contrary to Him, no matter how much this break may cost. It sees the obligation of unswerving fidelity to His love, no matter how difficult that fidelity may sometimes appear to be. Finally, it sees the need to rely completely on Him in perfect trust, abandoning our whole life into His hands and letting Him take care of us without our being able to see how He intends to do so. This is the genuine dimension of Christian faith.[8]

When the living Lord Jesus resides in and is vitally active within a Christian, He cannot and does not overlook the selfishness and sinfulness of a person's motivations, attitudes, and behavior. To do so would be to deny Himself, His character, the essential purpose of His Being.

Since the personal relationship the Christian has with Christ is a relational union that establishes the individual's spiritual identity as a Christ-one, the indwelling Christ must be allowed to express Himself in the Christian by overcoming all selfishness that is contrary to His character.

♥

*"All things are open and laid bare to the eyes of Him with Whom we have to do" (Heb. 4:13), and He will lovingly expose and root out all that is not consistent with Himself.*

Christianity is Christ, and true to Himself He will counter and overcome all that is contrary to His absolute character until He is "all in all" of the Christian's life.

This is the sure sign of being Christian – the Lord Jesus Christ functioning as Savior in the Christian, manifesting His "saving life" (Rom. 5:10) to "save us from our sins" (Matt. 1:21). To refuse this sanctifying work of Jesus Christ is to abort the objective of God's glorification in the Christian life, to sell our birthright for a "mess of pottage" (Gen. 25:29-34).

British missionary Norman Grubb explained,

Even when Christ has been welcomed within, that old self, largely unrecognized, will still reveal its presence in a thousand ways by self-will, self-importance, self-sufficiency, or by a self-consciousness, or a self-depreciation that paralyzes. God's Spirit has to take every forward-moving soul through a drastic process of self-exposure. That root of sin has to be looked in the face. Its presumptuous claim to be a sufficient source of wisdom and ability has to be exposed in its falsity.[9]

The subtleties of our selfishness seem to be endless. When we are angry, it is often a selfish response to being offended. When we insist on being happy, it is but a selfish desire to have everything "go our way." When we are bored, it may be evidence that we selfishly expect life to be constantly exciting. When we are critical, it may be a selfish expectation that others should be perfect.

When we worry or react in panic, it is often a selfish denial that God is capable of controlling the situation. When we are disappointed with our own failure and feel condemned, is it because we selfishly think we could have done it better?

When we snub another person and refuse to talk to them, we might selfishly think that the other person is not worth relating to or communicating with. When we talk too much, we selfishly clamor for attention and think that people should listen to us. When we are tardy, it may be because we selfishly think that others' time is not as important as ours, and they should wait until we decide to arrive.

When we overeat, is it because we selfishly think our tastes and hungers should be satisfied to the fullest? When we drink to excess, it is often because we selfishly think we can drown our pain, and ironically feel in control of the situation.

Our attempts to get rich are often evidence of our selfish trust in mammon.

When we ogle pornographic images, we selfishly think that titillating images can satisfy our desires for intimacy. Self-gratification pursues improper sexual activity outside of the God-ordained marriage relationship. We could go on and on.

♥

*Contemporary Christians are amazingly adept at glossing over and covering up their sin patterns.*

In the disavowal of "denial," they refuse to consider their selfish motivations. Many think that it impinges on their "spirituality" to admit weaknesses, inordinate cravings, fantasies, preoccupations, besetting sins, etc.

The unregenerate world is sometimes more honest in owning up to their obsessions, compulsions and addictions, as well as their phobias, denials and fears, as they gather together in accountability groups, sensitivity groups and anonymity groups and seek to deal with their destructive propensities by self-help and self-improvement programs.

Christians must face up to their selfishness patterns, without any attempts to minimize or rationalize, and without any delusion of their ability to overcome their sinful propensities by their own power and effort.

Sometimes Christians think they can keep their sins secret and hidden, at least from other Christians, if not from God (cf. Heb. 4:13). Behind closed doors they indulge their selfish sins, or even within their minds they engage in fantasies, rationalizing that if they do not "act out" externally, they have avoided sin.

Jesus explained that sin is internal before it is ever externalized, when He said, "Everyone who looks on a woman to lust for her has committed adultery with her already in his heart" (Matt. 5:28). When the will of man consents by saying, "I would if I could. I'm willing," the sin-decision has already been made by a volitional choice, constrained only by the unavailable opportunity.

Many Christians consider the sin in their lives only when distressing situations threaten. In situations of calamity, affliction, illness, or medical emergency, they vow and resolve to cease from their patterns of sin. They may be temporarily quieted within by such relinquishment to God's way in their lives, but it is often a temporary victory over their sinful tendencies, for when the ordeal is over, the sinful patterns break out again.

The same pattern is evident in those who address their sin only when "the sin has found them out" and their guilty actions have been exposed to those around them. Appearing contrite and ashamed, they vow to reform their behavior.

♥
_____ _____

*When we seek to deal with sin only because of the*
*consequences that are troubling us,*
*it is only a selfish desire to be relieved of the*
*consequences.*

_____

Self-selected categories of submitting our sinful
patterns to the sanctifying work of Jesus Christ are
another ploy that Christians often employ. We
conveniently compartmentalize our lives, thinking that
we can selectively offer one self-chosen area of
sinfulness to the saving function of the Savior, and
reserve others for another time. In this way we seek to
control our own sanctification, rather than allowing the
Lord Jesus Christ to control what He wants to do in our
lives.

Our pride knows no bounds in seeking to avoid
what Jesus Christ wants to do in dealing with our
selfishness. We are often blind to what is happening
within us when we tolerate selfish patterns, particularly
when God has revealed His desire to deal with them.

Our heart can "be hardened by the deceitfulness of
sin" (Heb. 3:13). Our conscience can be seared by
repetitive unwillingness to surrender to the Spirit. We
develop an indifference to God's desires, and
insensitivity to God's direction. We wonder why we do
not seem to have any constructive creativity of thought,
and do not participate in the joyous spontaneity of being
"used of God." Lack of comfort, peace, and rest leaves

us unsettled. The overflow of genuine Christian ministry is thwarted as we "quench the Spirit" (I Thess. 5:19).

# The "Flesh"

These patterns of sin within the Christian that we have been referring to are identified as the "flesh." Perhaps no other word in the Christian vocabulary has been more confounded and confused than the word "flesh" in reference to Christian behavior. This merits a closer look at how the writers of scripture, particularly Paul, use the word "flesh."

Centuries prior to Paul, the Greek language had used the word *sarx* to refer to the muscle or meat of living animals and human beings. They often associated the word with "flesh and blood" or "flesh and bones," as we still do today.

This close association with the physical body was transcended when the Greek philosopher Epicurus (341-270 B.C.) began to employ *sarx* as the "seat of desires," merging physical and psychological desires, especially in reference to pleasure and sensuality. *Sarx* was linked with *hedone*, in reference to the indulging of desires in selfish and sensate ways of moral corruption. Still today, Epicurianism and hedonism are used synonymously as the indulging of our desires in selfish pleasure.

For three hundred years the Greek word *sarx* had evolved with a connection not just to physicality, but also to the internal desires of man. So when Paul employed the word in the first century A.D., he used the whole range of then contemporary usages of the Greek word.

Sometimes he used *sarx* almost synonymously with the Greek word for "body," *soma* (cf. II Cor. 4:11; 12:7; Gal. 4:13). The meaning was expanded when Paul used *sarx* to refer to humanness or creatureliness (cf. Rom. 3:20; Gal. 2:16; I Tim. 3:16), and then to all that was earthly or worldly (cf. I Cor. 1:26). In conjunction with the usage in Genesis, Paul also referred to the "one flesh" of marital union (cf. Eph. 5:31).

In the widely debated passages where Paul used *sarx* in reference to Christian behavior, he utilized the meaning that had evolved in Greek philosophy from Epicurus onwards, referring to the selfish and sinful patterns within the desires of man (cf. Rom. 7:18,25; 8:4-13; 13:14; Gal. 5:16-24; Eph. 2:3).

To understand this background of Greek word usage will prevent us from the over-generalization that indicates that Paul uses the word "flesh" in terms of the physicality of the body of human beings. When Christian interpreters so define "flesh," they easily fall prey to the Greek dualism of regarding the body as evil and the spirit as good.

There is nothing in scripture that regards the physicality or corporeality of the physical body (*soma*) as evil, bad, wrong, or sinful in itself. On the other hand, there is definitely an ascription of sinfulness, selfishness and evil to the word *sarx* as Paul sometimes employs it.

Paul does not fall prey to the Greek dualism of physicality vs. spirituality (*sarx* vs. *pneuma, nous,* or *logos*), but he does set up an either-or antithesis of "flesh" vs. Spirit (*sarx* vs. *Pneuma*) in behavioral conflict. These are not substantive entities, but behavioral impulses that are connected with human desires.

Before we attempt to define Paul's behavioral usage of the word "flesh," it will be instructive to consider what the "flesh" is not, and what the "flesh" is.

The "flesh" is not related to one's spiritual condition, and is not equivalent to spiritual depravity. The "flesh" is not to be personified as the presence of Satan in the individual, whether non-Christian or Christian. The "flesh" is not substantive or partitive, meaning that it is not an entity, like a "hunk of evil," within the individual. The "flesh" is not a generative source of evil within the individual.

The "flesh" is not inherent or intrinsic to humanity, even fallen humanity. The "flesh" is not nascent or congenital, meaning that no person is born with the "flesh," and there are no hereditary patterns of fleshliness.

The "flesh" is not eradicated at conversion or during the Christian life. The "flesh" does not become better or reformed. The "flesh" is not to be identified with, equated with, or used as a synonym of "inherent sin, sin-principle, law of sin, old man, old self, old nature, sin-nature, self-nature, Adam-nature, human nature," etc.

Conversely, the "flesh" is related to behavior, and relates to the psychological function of the soul. The "flesh" is related to the "desires" of man within the soul, allowing for the phrases "fleshly desires," and "desires of the flesh" (cf. Rom. 13:14; Gal. 5:24; Eph. 2:3; I Peter 2:11). The "flesh" refers to how these desires are patterned toward selfishness and sinfulness within the soul.

The "flesh" patterns are developed throughout the experiences of our lives, and are individualized in idiosyncratic patterns of selfish action and/or reaction. Some of these "flesh" patterns become deep-seated habituated patterns of addictive, obsessive, and compulsive behavior, sometimes called "besetting sins" or "strongholds of sin." All human beings have developed these patterns of "fleshly desires," with the sole exception of Jesus Christ.

———— ♥ ————

*Every Christian still has these "flesh" patternings*
*of selfishness and sinfulness in the desires of his soul,*
*even though completely regenerated spiritually,*

*and these patterns and propensities*
*will remain throughout*
*the Christian's earthly life.*

As "flesh" is connected with desires, it is necessary to recognize that God creates every person with a full set of God-given human desires in their soul. These desires are amoral; they are not wrong in themselves. They are God-given behavioral conduits – intended to be pipelines that allow God's character to be expressed in human behavior.

Examples of such needs, drives and desires are: the desire to be loved and accepted, to belong, to be nurtured, sustained, and provided for. We have a desire for security, order, communication, belief, meaning and purpose, contentment, excitement, uniqueness, and identity.

In addition we have a desire for freedom, worship, appreciation of beauty, creativity, motivation, and responsibility. We even have a desire to work and achieve, a desire for significance, a desire to possess, to give, to serve, and a desire for hope and expectancy.

The basic desires to eat, drink, sleep, and for sexual expression must also be included. There is nothing wrong with any of these God-given desires.

The Greek language had two primary words for "desire." The first of these was *epithumia*, which meant "to be moved upon, to urge upon, or to have passion upon." The second word was *epipotheo*, which meant "to yearn upon, to experience upon (usually from outside)."

Our God-given desires could be "urged upon" or "yearned upon" by the Spirit of God, or they could be "urged upon" or "yearned upon" by the tempting influence of Satan as he seeks to fulfill the God-given desires in God-forbidden ways.

Though every person is born with clear, pure, and sinless desires, our desires are "urged upon" and "yearned upon" by "the spirit that works in the sons of disobedience" (Eph. 2:2). The unregenerate – "dead in trespasses and sins" (Eph. 2:1,5), and "slaves to sin" (Rom. 6:6) – have only this "operating system" to work with. They are caught in the vortex of satanically inspired self-orientation that inevitably develops selfish and sinful patterns of action and reaction in the desires of their soul.

The desires of every person become bent, warped, twisted, and kinked in individuated patterns of selfishness and sinfulness – personalized patterns of selfishly indulgent desires. While the particular warp of the various desires, and the strength of the selfish twists, is unique and different in every person, there is no doubt that some selfish patterns of desires have more social consequences than others.

Everyone seems to have one or more deep-seated and habituated patterns that become "besetting sins" (cf. Heb. 12:1) which they cannot conquer, try as they might.

When an individual becomes a Christian by spiritual regeneration, and the Spirit of Christ comes to live in the spirit of that individual (Rom. 8:9), their spiritual condition is complete (Col. 2:10) and "all has become new" (II Cor. 5:17). However, the "flesh" – the selfish and sinful patterns of action and reaction in the desires of the soul – remains in the new Christian. This sets up the conflict whereby "the flesh sets its desires against the Spirit, and the Spirit against the flesh" (Gal. 5:17).

This is not a conflict of contrasting natures in the Christian, but a motivational conflict between the old patterns of selfish action and reaction and the prompting of the Spirit of Christ to express His character in our behavior.

In like manner as Paul explained that we are "dead to sin" (Rom. 6:11) and "freed from sin" (Rom. 6:7,18,22), he also declares that "those who belong to Christ Jesus have crucified the flesh with its passions and desires" (Gal. 5:24), and "the members of our earthly body are dead to immorality, impurity, passion, evil desire, and greed" (Col. 3:5).

---------- ♥ ----------

*Christians are "no longer in the flesh" (Rom. 7:5; 8:8,9), in the sense that they are enslaved to the satanically inspired "operating system" that makes them "slaves of sin" (Rom. 6:6,17) and "sinful passions" (Rom. 7:5).*

Converted "from the dominion of Satan to God" (Acts 26:18), the "flesh" patternings, energized as they are by the tempter, have no legitimate claim or mastery over our behavior as Christians – for we have received the greater power (cf. I John 4:4) of the Lord Jesus Christ within our spirit. Christians are "under no obligation" (Rom. 8:12) to respond by means of the selfish action and reaction patterns of the "flesh," but are instead to "make no provision for the flesh" (Rom. 13:14) by capitulating and catering to those selfish desires.

Underlying the particular selfish bent of our desires is a twisted mind-set that pervades, and provides a selfish motivating perspective to the self-concerns of our "flesh."

All fallen men, alienated from God in their unregeneracy, have developed the premise that they are an "independent self" that is inherently capable of self-generating character and behavior that is self-righteous, and that by means of their own self-sufficiency and self-reliance. This presupposition of human potential to perform and produce all that man needs is the humanistic lie that fallaciously prompts man with a self-motivation to "be all he can be."

When an individual becomes a Christian, this fallacious humanistic mind-set of being an "independent self" is the most difficult part of the "flesh" to overcome, because we cling tenaciously to this fallacy of auto-generative human performance and self-effort, even transferring this thesis to the alleged Christian ability to live the Christian life by performing in accord with God's expectations.

This foundational premise of all fleshly thinking can only be overcome as the Christian submits to the Spirit of Christ within, allowing Him to generate His character expressed through our desires in godly behavior. When that liberating transitional process begins to take place, we can experience the freedom that God intended for man.

It is not the responsibility of the Christian to identify and fight against the "flesh" mind-set and patterns. That would of necessity entail the self-effort that is intrinsic to the selfishness of the "flesh." In the midst of the motivational conflict of the "flesh" and the Spirit, Paul advises that "the Spirit sets its desires against the flesh" (Gal. 5:17).

———— ♥ ————

*The "battle is the Lord's" (I Sam. 17:47);*
*for the living Christ is the only Victor Who can*
*overcome sinfulness and selfishness*
*in the Christian life.*

Evangelical Christian teaching has often failed to understand this basic premise of divine action in the Christian life. Admonishing Christians not to "walk according to the flesh" (Rom. 8:4) nor to "live according to the flesh" (Rom. 8:12,13) by manifesting the "deeds of the flesh" (Gal. 5:19-21), religious teachers often advise the human resolve of commitment to overcome the "flesh" and live the Christian life.

In a dyslexic reversion of Paul's gospel of grace, they read Galatians 5:16 backwards: "Do not carry out the desires of the flesh, and you will be walking in the Spirit." What an abominable mistranslation.

Paul says, "Walk by the Spirit, and you will not carry out the desires of the flesh, . . . for the Spirit sets its desires against the flesh" (Gal. 5:16,17). By the indwelling presence of the Spirit of Christ (cf. Rom. 8:9; Gal. 4:6; II Tim. 1:14), the Christian is "led of the Spirit" (Rom. 8:14; Gal. 5:18) in order to "walk by the

Spirit" (Rom. 8:4; Gal. 5:16,25) and manifest the "fruit of the Spirit" (Gal. 5:22,23).

As a final statement about the "flesh," it is important to note that it is not the "desires of the flesh" which tempt us to act out in sinful behavior. The patterns of selfish and sinful action and reaction are well entrenched in our soul, but they have no inherent power to energize and actuate sinful behavior. The Evil One is the only energizing source of the evil character that actuates sinful expression.

Many English translations of James 1:14 appear to indicate that "we are tempted when we are enticed by our own desire." A more careful translation will read, "Each one is tempted (by the tempter), being enticed and lured under his own desire." Satan, the tempter, goes fishing under our idiosyncratic patterns of fleshly desires, which he knows so well, seeking to attract and ensnare us to make a choice that will employ his evil character via those old patterns of selfish action and reaction. There is nothing in scripture that indicates that the Christian is self-tempted by the desires of the "flesh," by an old-nature, or by some evil "self."

## "Self"

In conjunction with the sinful patterns of the "flesh," religious teachers often admonish Christians of the necessity of dealing with the "self." Some religionists make it appear that there is an evil "boogey man" lurking down in a person's psyche, or a "dirty old man" hiding in a cave deep inside of us. "Self" is often

45

identified with an alleged "old man" within, or a residual "old nature." What is this "self" that is so often alluded to in religious teaching?

Sometimes we are admonished to accept ourselves, love ourselves, control ourselves, and behave ourselves. Conversely, we are encouraged to surrender ourselves, humble ourselves, deny ourselves, and die to "self." This abundance of self-talk creates an ambiguity that leaves Christians scratching their heads about how they are to consider themselves and what they are to do with themselves.

We must attempt a clarification of how the word "self" is used in the English language. As a word that stands alone it is of relatively modern origin, being a truncation of the word "selfishness" or of the pronominal references to "myself, yourself, himself," etc., referring to a person or individual. Current linguistic usages of the word "self" can be separated into the following five categories:

## (1) **Personal identity**

Who am I? Many have sought to find the basis of their identity in personal abilities (humanism), personal associations (socialism), and personal acquisitions (materialism), but these provide only a fleeting sense of identity that can fall prey to the circumstances of life. A more permanent basis of personal identity must be established at the spiritual core of our being. The Christian's identity is established in identification and union with the living Lord Jesus, whereby he becomes a "Christ-one," a Christian.

## (2) **Personal individuality**

Every person is distinctive and unique – myself distinguished from yourself. We are not Xerox copies that think the same and act the same. Even when we become Christians by the receipt of the Spirit of Christ within our spirit, we still retain personal individuality. Just think how monotonous the church would be if there were absolute similitude and conformity. An old truism states, "Variety is the spice of life." We have varying personalities, which are to some extent patterned by our idiosyncratic patterns of selfishness and sinfulness in the "flesh."

## (3) **Personal embodiment**

We are not disembodied spirits darting around in a "spooky" or "ghostly" interaction. Every human has a physical body that is the "house" we live in. It would be a very superficial view of mankind to propose that the primary essence of a person was their body, for this would fail to take into account the identity and individuality of the person who lives in that body. But there is nothing inherently evil or sinful about our bodies, and they are not to be regarded as "prison-houses" of the real "self," as Greek dualism advocated.

## (4) **Personal interest**

Man is not inherently sinful or selfish; but the egocentric character of the one who declared, "I will be like the Most High God" (Isa. 14:14), has invaded fallen humanity. "The spirit that works in the sons of disobedience" (Eph. 2:2) has caused his character of self-orientation and self-concern to pervade the desires of our soul, creating patterns of selfishness and sinfulness. Paul advised the Philippian Christians, "Do nothing from selfishness . . . do not look out for your own personal interests" (Phil. 2:3,4).

## (5) **Personal resource**

The Evil One suggested to original man, "You, too, can be like God" (Gen. 3:5), introducing the lie that man could self-determine good and evil apart from the character of God. Fallen man has accepted the humanistic fallacy that man can be his own god, the cause of his own effects and the solution to his own problems.

♥

*God created man as a derivative and contingent being, always dependent by receptivity from a spirit source.*

The fallacious thesis of "personal resource" is that man is an autonomous self-generating, self-actuating, self-achieving being – an "independent self." There is no such thing as "personal resource." It is a lie!

With the foregoing categories in mind, which "self" is the Christian to deny? We must not disavow our spiritual identity, our personal individuality, or our physical embodiment, but we can disavow the possibility of any personal resource of "independent self." The intent of Jesus' admonition to "deny yourself" (Matt. 16:24; Mark 8:34; Luke 9:23) was obviously that we are to disallow the selfishness of personal interest.

Which "self" are the religious teachers encouraging Christians to crucify or die to? To die to our spiritual identity in Christ would be apostasy. Surely we do not want to exterminate our personal individuality. To crucify our personal embodiment would be to commit suicide. Since personal resource is but a fabricated "straw man," it cannot be put to death.

The only possible meaning of their unbiblical inculcations is that they are suggesting that Christians terminate their selfishness, but this is often cast as another religious performance technique of self-effort, a masochistic attempt at self-crucifixion of selfishness.

When religious teachers refer to "self," they are often using the term as a synonym for the "flesh" patternings of selfishness and sinfulness. On many occasions, though, they have lapsed into an "evangelical humanism" that subtly accepts the thesis of "personal resource," explaining that the unregenerate individual has "ego" or "self" on the throne of their life, and that an alleged "carnal Christian" reverts to behaving out of self-resource. When they operate from this false premise, their admonitions to "deny self" or "die to self" become the absurdity of denying or crucifying a non-existent apparition that is but a logical fallacy.

# S. E. L. F.

The fleshly "personal interest" patterns in the desires of our soul can form bundles that are identified as personality or individuality characteristics. When the selfish and sinful patterns of our fleshly desires collect into pattern-bundles, we can observe four distinct categories of how individuals express their selfishness. Because these categories represent generalized groups of selfish expression, we will identify them as the "S" pattern-bundle, the "E" pattern-bundle, the "L" pattern-bundle, and the "F" pattern-bundle.

As graphically illustrated in Addendum B, the S.E.L.F. pattern-bundles of selfishness are placed in four quadrants. The two axes that separate the quadrants represent contrasts of pace and priority, energy and orientation, or activity and direction. The two quadrants to the left of the vertical axis represent pattern-bundles that are independently task-oriented, while the two quadrants to the right of the vertical axis represent pattern-bundles that are relationally people-oriented. The two quadrants above the horizontal axis represent pattern-bundles that are active, self-motivated change agents, while the two quadrants below the horizontal axis represent pattern-bundles that are reserved, self-conscious, and introspective.

Individuals with an **"S" pattern-bundle** of fleshly selfishness have a high-energy task-orientation. They crave self-significance as they seek self-success by means of their own self-sufficiency. Their greatest fear is that they will fail. They exude self-confidence as they assert, "I can do it. Just give me the project, I will

organize the tools and the people and get the job done."
In the process they are competitive, confrontational,
assertive, and bossy. They demand that others assist in
their endeavors, and declare, "We're going to do it my
way, even if we have to bend some rules to get it done."
They are firm believers in "the end justifies the means."
They are strong-willed, impatient, and proud, wanting
others to see and admire their accomplishments and
achievements. Because everything is a "project to
complete," they tend to view their Christian life as a
project, and seek techniques to make the Christian life
work.

Those with an **"E" pattern-bundle** of fleshly
selfishness have a high-energy people-orientation. They
crave the self-stimulation of exciting involvement with
other people. Their greatest fear is loneliness and
isolation. They are extroverted, energetic, expressive,
and entertaining. In the process of this self-exposure,
they desire to be noticed by others, so they often spend
an inordinate amount of time on physical externals of
"image" and "impressions." They want to be the center
of attention, the "life of the party," so they often display
themselves as people-pleasing show-offs. They demand
to be heard, and seem to talk all the time, dominating
most discussions. They will often exaggerate and
embellish the subject at hand in order to make things
appear more exciting. They will often promise more
than they can deliver, and are often undependable, but
quick to make excuses and blame others for their
failures. Their approach to the Christian life is to seek a
social interaction of exciting fellowship.

Those with an **"L" pattern-bundle** of fleshly selfishness have a less-active, more pensive people-orientation. They crave a calm, serene social environment, wanting everything to remain as it is in the status quo. Their greatest fear is the unknown of change. They stubbornly hold on to what they are comfortable with in their "comfort zone." They hate surprises, wanting to know what is going to happen in advance, and wanting everything predictable. Though they dislike it when people mess up their plans and routine, they are not likely to tell you because they "stuff" their feelings and stifle communication. Eschewing all conflict, they do not want to offend anyone or "ruffle any feathers." Overly worried about what others think of them, they are often compliant and complacent, taking the path of least resistance and being too quick to compromise. They desire a Christian life of conservative traditionalism in a group where everyone gets along with one another.

Those with an **"F" pattern-bundle** of fleshly selfishness have a reserved and pensive task-orientation. They crave accuracy and correctness, demanding what is "right and proper." They intensely seek to know all that they can know, in an attempt to get everything figured out and know all the facts. Their greatest fear is the embarrassment of being wrong, or not knowing the answer. Believing that there is a "right way to do everything," they self-righteously seek to be right in everything, demanding the highest standards for themselves and for others. In the process they are often hard to please, critical, faultfinding, and censorious, sometimes with a "know it all" attitude of superiority. They can be suspicious and distrusting, skeptical of anything they have not figured out logically. They tend to view the Christian life as a rigid alignment of doctrinal accuracy and behavioral propriety.

These S.E.L.F. pattern-bundles simply reveal how different individuals tend to function naturally in the selfish action and reaction patterns of their soul's desires. They become, however, the basis by which persons are "known" by others, the basis by which the world evaluates a person's individuality or personality, and even the false basis of personal identity.

Even Christians, when they seek to excuse and justify their behavior, will often say, "Well, that's just the real me. That's the way I am." Even when advised of their true spiritual identity in Christ, some Christians will retort, "But you just don't know how bad the 'real me' is."

♥

*When Christians use these patterns of selfishness*
*as the false basis of their identity,*
*they are basing their identity on their soul-condition*
*rather than on their spirit-condition,*
*on their sinfulness rather than on the Savior.*

It is a sad state of affairs when people base their identity on their selfish "flesh" patterns, believing that they are helpless victims of a fateful natural selection of personalities. When Christians fall prey to this irresponsible escapist thinking, it simply reveals how uninformed they are of their spiritual identity in Christ, and all that is theirs "in Christ."

These S.E.L.F. bundles of selfish "flesh" patterns in the desires of our soul do not constitute who we are, but merely the grouping of our "fleshly desires" that the Spirit of Christ sets His desires against (Gal. 5:17) and seeks to overcome by the expression of His divine character.

Do these S.E.L.F. groupings correspond to the Hippocratic body fluid variances, the temperament types of choleric, sanguine, phlegmatic and melancholy, or the other personality profiles that have become popular? Though there may be similarities, the fundamental difference is in their presuppositions that the personality traits constitute one's identity, and that there are inherent strengths and "good points" to each personality, necessitating that you "accentuate your positive, eliminate your negatives, and live up to your self-potential."

The humanistic premises of self-potential must be rejected. The apostle Paul explained, "In me, that is in my flesh, dwells no good thing" (Rom. 7:18), and since the S.E.L.F. categories are but bundles of our fleshly patterns of selfishness, we must submit to the work of the Lord Jesus Christ within us to overcome these natural propensities by expressing His life and character through our desires.

# 3

## The Positive Swallows Up
## the Negative

Much of the emphasis of religion is on the
prohibitions of avoiding certain sinful activities in order
to engage in other pious activities that will result in
what God wants in our lives. The "thou shalt nots" are
alleged to lay the groundwork for the "thou shalts."

The fallacy behind all such religious incentive is
the false premise of an "independent self" that is
capable of overcoming sin, and consequently capable of
manifesting godliness. Impossible!

Writing to the Colossians, Paul revealed the
impotence of religious prohibitions:

If you have died with Christ to the elementary
principles of the world, why, as if you were living in
the world, do you submit yourself to decrees, such

as, "Do not handle, do not taste, do not touch!" – in accordance with the commandments and teachings of men? These are matters which have, to be sure, the appearance of wisdom in self-made religion and self-abasement and severe treatment of the body, but are of no value against fleshly indulgence (Col. 2:20-23).

Notice that Paul declares that the "do nots" of religious prohibition "are of no value against fleshly indulgence." How much good do the religious "thou shalt nots" do? None! They are exercises in futility. How much good do the "thou shalt" commandments of self-made religion do? None! They are equally as futile in effecting the manifestation of the character of God in man.

But religion never gives up in their admonitions for self-reform. Century after century the preachers have admonished their parishioners to "be not conformed to this world," without telling them the good news that if they are "transformed by the renewing of their mind" (Rom. 12:2) they will not have to concern themselves with being conformed to the world.

Innumerable have been the temperance sermons chastising listeners to "be not drunk with wine," without advising them that when they are "filled with the Spirit" (Eph. 5:18) the control of the Lord Jesus Christ will supersede any escapism into drunkenness. Urging zealous Christians to "resist the devil, and he will flee from you," the teachers failed to explain that when a Christian "submits himself to God" (James 4:7) the devil is resisted by the only One competent to resist him.

Many have made the call of Jesus — to "deny yourself, take up the cross, and follow Me" — into a commandment of self-resolve and self-effort, without recognizing that when we "follow Jesus" in utter abandonment, we will consequently be denying ourselves and taking up the cross (Luke 9:23). The religious dyslexia of admonishing people to "not carry out the desires of the flesh, in order to walk in the Spirit," rather than encouraging people to "walk in the Spirit, and you will not carry out the desires of the flesh" (Gal. 5:16), has already been noted.

The religious cause-and-effect reasoning that sin must be overcome so Christ can rule as Lord is utterly false. We do not have to first empty ourselves in order to be filled with Christ. We do not have to excise the cancer of sin in order to experience a healthy expression of Christ's life. We do not have to die in order to live – Jesus already took care of that!

—————— ♥ ——————

*The good news of the gospel is that
life overcomes death, light overcomes darkness, good
overcomes evil, and love overcomes selfishness,
because God overcomes Satan.*

"Greater is He Who is in you, than he who is in the world" (I John 4:4). Jesus is the Overcomer.

The process of "dealing with sin" is not the *requirement* but the *evidence* of Christ's Lordship in our lives. Jesus said, "You shall know the Truth (Himself – John 14:6), and the Son will set you free" (John 8:28,32), inclusive of all our selfish and sinful patterns of the "flesh."

Religion is "put out of business" when the gospel of God's grace activity in Jesus Christ reveals how "the positive swallows up the negative." Oh, the liberating freedom of understanding that godliness swallows up sinfulness, and the "fruit of the Spirit" (Gal. 5:22,23) will swallow up the "deeds of the flesh" (Gal. 5:19-21).

## The Process *Positiva*

The positive side of the sanctification process – what we are calling the "process *positiva*" – sets in motion the negative side of the sanctification process, the "process *negativa*."

Once again, it is important to remember that salvation is more than a static conversion event of a punctiliar regeneration experience. Salvation is the entire process of "being made safe" from the dysfunction of "the spirit working in the sons of disobedience" (Eph. 2:2) to the functional manifestation of the life of Jesus Christ in our mortal bodies (II Cor. 4:10,11). Salvation is inclusive of the process of sanctification.

Christians are "chosen of God, holy and beloved" (Col. 3:12), "created in holiness" (Eph. 4:24) by the presence of the Holy One (cf. Acts 2:27; 3:12; 13:35), the "Spirit of holiness, Jesus Christ our Lord" (Rom. 1:4) within our spirit. We are "saints" (Eph. 1:18; 4:12), "holy ones," engaged in the process of behaving like who we have become. Progressive sanctification is that process of "perfecting holiness in the fear of God," and thus "cleansing ourselves from all defilement of flesh and spirit" (II Cor. 7:1) by His overcoming action.

There is no doubt that there is a process of growth in the Christian life. This is not, however, to be conceived as our getting better, growing stronger, or growing "more spiritual." The growth process is the process whereby we "grow in the grace and knowledge of our Lord and Savior, Jesus Christ" (II Pet. 3:18), and "grow up in all respects into Him Who is the head, even Christ" (Eph. 4:15).

───────── ♥ ─────────

*We submit to the daily process of allowing "our inner man to be renewed day by day" (II Cor. 4:16) to participate in a growing manifestation of Christ's life.*

Paul's plea for the Galatians was that "Christ be formed in them" (Gal. 4:19). This was not a desire for regenerative new birth, for they were already Christians, but Paul labored for the inner formation of Christ's life in the Galatian Christians that they might be "conformed to the image of the Son" (Rom. 8:29). Just as the formation of the embryo in the womb is a process, so the formation of Christ's character in the Christian is an ongoing process.

59

John Wesley correctly explained the process of sanctification as the restoration or renewal of the image of God in man. The *imago dei,* the "image of God," is not an image by representation or an image by reflection, but an image by the very reality of the presence of God in man for the purpose of making visible, or visaging, the character of God in the behavior of man to the glory of God.

Jesus Christ "is the image of the invisible God" (Col. 1:15; II Cor. 4:4), the only means of making visible the character of the invisible God and "conforming us to His image" (Rom. 8:29). Although the Christian is initially "sanctified" (cf. I Cor. 1:2; 6:11; Heb. 10:14) in spiritual regeneration, we continue in the process of sanctification whereby "Christ our sanctification" (I Cor. 1:30) sets us apart to manifest His holy character in our behavior.

## The Process *Negativa*

Whereas the "process *positiva*" is the positive side of growing in the formation of God's holy character in Christian behavior, the "process *negativa*" is the process of negating all expression of sinful character that is contrary to Christ, the propensities toward which have been patterned into the selfish action and reaction patterns of our "flesh."

Having already asserted that "the positive swallows up the negative," we can, nonetheless, examine some of the processes (or metaphors seeking to explain the process) whereby sin is dealt with in the Christian life.

Since religion focuses almost exclusively on the development of formulas and procedures for the eradication of sin, one must be constantly on guard to avoid allowing discussion of the "process *negativa*" to degenerate into consideration of religious performance techniques for dealing with sin.

Numerous explanations of the "process *negativa*" have been proffered throughout Christian history. We will construct a brief list of several of these:

## (1) **The purgative process**

Recognizing the need to purge sinful unrighteousness from the Christian's life, many writers developed elaborate theories of purgation. Beginning with Evagrius Ponticus, and further developed by St. John of the Cross and St. Teresa of Avila, the "three ways of spirituality" were identified as (a) the purgative way, (b) the illuminative way, and (c) the unitive way.

The "purgative way" was usually inculcation to self-purgation through various self-disciplines in order to develop "purity of heart" and "union with God." Later emphasis on the need of indulgences and penances for present purgation and the place of an intermediate place of purgatory for future purgation developed the explanation of the "purgative process" even more. The Protestant reaction to "works" of performance for righteousness caused them to eschew mention of purgation in lieu of other explanations.

## (2) The purification process

God's absolute character of purity desires to purify His people from the impurity of their selfish and sinful "flesh" patterns. Elaborate religious purification rites like those practiced in the Judaism of the first century do not accomplish such inner purification, however. The means by which we "purify our hearts" (James 4:8) is to allow Jesus "to purify for Himself a people for His own possession, zealous for good deeds" (Titus 2:14). Divine purity must drive out impurity, just as God drove out the inhabitants of Canaan for the Israelite peoples.

## (3) The refining process

Just as the smelter reveals the dross, the base, and the impurities in the ore, it is argued that the divine furnace of God's purifying love will burn away that which is base and impure in our lives. "Our God is a consuming fire" (Heb. 12:29), writes the author to the Hebrews, and "the spirit of burning" (Isa. 4:4) will "test us by fire" (I Peter 1:7). "He will sit as a smelter and purifier of silver" (Mal. 3:13), "refining us as silver is refined" (Ps. 66:10).

Notice that it is God's action of refining, not our action of self-refinement.

## (4) The cleansing process

The filth of our selfishness and sin requires the cathartic action of the Spirit of God. This is not accomplished by religious ceremonial cleansings, but "the blood of Christ cleanses our conscience from dead works, to serve the living God" (Heb.

9:14). The "perfecting of holiness by the fear of God" enacts the "cleansing from all defilement of flesh and spirit" (II Cor. 7:1). "He is faithful and just to cleanse us from all unrighteousness" (I John 1:9).

### (5) **The healing process**

Although religion has often emphasized ministries of physical healings, we must not overlook the necessity of psychological healing among God's people. The diseases and infectious cancers in our soul need more than the salves of psychological techniques. They need the work of the Great Physician Who alone can restore health to our desires and behavioral function.

### (6) **The finishing process**

By the "finished work" of Christ (cf. John 19:30) everything is set in motion to accomplish all that God intends to do in man. The finished work of redemption continues in the finishing work of restoration. Christians participate in God's "finishing school" as He desires that we be "perfect and complete, lacking in nothing" (James 1:4).

### (7) **The overcoming process**

Evil is overcome by good (Rom. 12:21). The overcoming of our tendencies, propensities and habits of selfishness will not be achieved through self-effort at personal housecleaning. The Christian who overcomes (cf. Rev. 2:7–3:21) will do so only by submitting to the One Who has already "overcome the world" (John 16:33) and desires to continue His overcoming action in Christians' lives (cf. I John 5:4,5).

## (8) **The discipline process**

"Those whom the Lord loves He disciplines" (Heb. 12:5), and only illegitimate children escape divine discipline, the author of Hebrews advises us. "He disciplines us for our good, that we might share His holiness" and participate in "the peaceful fruit of righteousness" (Heb. 12:10,11). Discipline is not to be viewed as punishment or chastisement, nor is discipline to be identified as difficult and unpleasant circumstances. Discipline is God's process of forming us into the disciples He wants us to be, ever following and learning of the Lord Jesus Christ.

## (9) **The process of resignation**

Many writers have encouraged Christians to surrender all defiant self-will by submissive resignation to God's will in their lives. The abandoning of self-will will never be accomplished by self-will, however, for our selfish desires clamor for attention and expression. Resignation should not be understood as passive acquiescence that fails to recognize the constant responsibility of Christian faith that is receptive to God's activity.

## (10) **The process of poverty**

Since the selfishness of our desires often includes the desire to acquire and possess material things, as well as knowledge, and position, etc., Christians are often advised to engage in a process of personal impoverishment that repudiates all acquisition and ownership. "Blessed are the poor in spirit" (Matt. 5:3), Jesus taught, but this does not imply that a self-imposed state of material impoverishment will necessarily beget godliness.

## (11) **The process of humiliation**

In like manner as the Son of God "humbled Himself, becoming obedient unto death" (Phil. 2:6), Christians have been urged to overcome pride and self-exaltation in their souls by humbly accepting disappointment, perplexity, and failure. The experience of being humiliated does not in itself remove our self-concern, though, for often it fosters additional self-resolve.

## (12) **The process of mortification**

The English word "mortify" means "to put to death." Writing to the Romans, Paul states, "If by the Spirit you are putting to death (KJV – "do mortify") the deeds of the body, you will live" (Rom. 8:13). Too often, though, religious admonitions of mortification have encouraged a subjection or denial of bodily passions and appetites by abstinence or self-inflicted pain and discomfort. Owing to the abundance of instruction to mortify oneself by the self-crucifixion of "dying to self," we will devote a separate section to that subject.

## (13) **The process of suffering**

The apostle Paul sought to "know Jesus, and the fellowship of His sufferings, being conformed to His death" (Phil. 3:10). He "rejoiced in his sufferings" (Col. 1:24), counting it a privilege "to suffer for His sake" (Phil. 1:29), believing that "we suffer with Him in order that we may be glorified with Him" (Rom. 8:17).

Affliction, sorrow, and suffering are not to be sought as an end in themselves, but they are circumstances that God can use to bring us to the end of ourselves and to the recognition of our inability.

Many have mistakenly maintained that when St. John of the Cross wrote of *The Dark Night of the Soul*, he was extolling suffering in some kind of "spirituality *de noir*." He was not. The "dark nights of the soul" are those times when we are "in the dark" concerning what Christ is doing in our lives in various situations, and we are forced to "walk by faith, not by sight" (II Cor. 5:7). The darkness is when we do not understand what is going on, and we experience "lights out" on all our humanistic enlightenment ideas of human potential and solution. In that darkness we realize that God is more of a mystery that our finite understanding will ever comprehend or figure out.

There are many other concepts that have been utilized by well-meaning Christians to explain the necessity of "dealing with sin" in the Christian life. Concepts like brokenness, abandonment, self-limitation, self-minimizing, detachment, pruning, etc. All of these processes used to explain the "process *negativa*" have been misused to encourage self-enacted religious techniques and "disciplines" to accomplish what only God can do. When they become merely forms of "self-abasement and severe treatment of the body," they are, in Paul's words, "of no value against fleshly indulgence" (Col. 2:23).

## The Process of Death and Crucifixion

The experiential application of the symbol of the cross to the negating of the selfish patterns of sin in the soul of the Christian could have been another of the processes noted above, but due to its most popular usage we will consider it separately as "the process of death and crucifixion."

In much Christian literature through the centuries the "process *negativa*" is broadly referred to as "the way of the cross," or "the work of the cross," with its corollaries of "crucifying self," "dying to self," and "putting self to death." It has become so popular that any questioning of the legitimacy of this process is regarded akin to sacrilege.

———— ♥ ————

*The physical death of Jesus Christ on the execution instrument of a Roman cross would have been just another expedient crucifixion were it not for the fact that the One being crucified was the incarnate Son of God.*

Having emptied Himself of all prerogative of divine action in order to become a man, capable of death, "Jesus humbled Himself and became obedient to the point of death, even death on a cross" (Phil. 2:7,8).

The death of the divine Savior on the cross of Calvary was a singular, once and for all event (Heb. 7:27; 10:10; I Peter 3:18), the redemptive sacrifice of the perfect Son of God taking the death consequences of the sin of humanity upon Himself in order to restore His divine life to receptive men. We emphasize the singularity and completeness of the redemptive crucifixion of Jesus on the cross because any reference to extended experiential prolongation of "the way of the cross" can risk impinging upon the finality of Christ's objective, historical, finished work on the cross.

There is also a once and for all subjective implication of the cross for every Christian. "You have died and your life is hidden with Christ in God" (Col. 3:3), Paul told the Colossians. When we are spiritually regenerated our "old man has been crucified with Christ" (Rom. 6:6). "I have been crucified with Christ; it is no longer I who live, but Christ lives in me" (Gal. 2:20), Paul declares.

───────── ♥ ─────────

*This subjective identification with the death of Christ occurs at regeneration, and does not occur repetitively as an experiential process of sanctification.*

When the "old man" has been crucified with Christ, and we are a "new creature in Christ" (II Cor. 5:17), we are "dead to sin" (Rom. 6:2,11), "dead to the law" (Rom. 7:3,4; Gal. 2:19), and "have crucified the flesh" (Gal. 5:24), indicating that the authority of these modalities has been terminated, disallowing any legitimacy of their function in our Christian life.

In what sense, then, might there be any experiential "application of the cross" or "dying to self" as a continuous process in the Christian life? Many have misused Paul's statements, "I die daily" (I Cor. 15:31), "we are being put to death all day long" (Rom. 8:36), and "we are constantly being delivered over to death for Jesus' sake" (II Cor. 4:11), as texts to justify such, but contextually these can only be applied to Paul's physical persecution whereby he was being beaten and battered unto death, and do not refer to a continuing crucifixion within the Christian.

What is the import of Jesus' comments about "taking up," "bearing," or "carrying" a cross (Matt. 10:38; 16:24; Mark 8:34; Luke 9:23; 14:27)? On three different occasions Jesus made general metaphorical comments about the action of bearing a cross unto crucifixion. As His comments were prior to His own crucifixion, there is no reference here to the cross of Christ, but only to the common action that preceded Roman crucifixion, i.e., the condemned carrying their own execution instrument to the location of their execution.

Those who heard Jesus' statements surely understood that a complete following of Jesus would mean the denial of self-concerns of personal interest, even to the point of being willing to accept the stigma of a condemned criminal carrying his cross to the place of crucifixion. Proper exegesis does not allow, however, for any experiential extension of an inward application of Christ's cross.

In his epistle to the Roman Christians, Paul writes, "If you are living according to the flesh, you must die; but if by the Spirit you are putting to death the deeds of the body, you will live" (Rom. 8:13). When Paul says, "you must die," is this an inculcation to experiential death in the Christian's life? It does not appear to be so. If Christians are living or behaving according to the selfish and sinful patterning in the desires of their soul, then they will certainly and inevitably express character and behavior that is devoid of the character of divine life. Their behavioral manifestation will "bring forth death" (James 1:15), expressive of "dead works" (Heb. 6:1; 9:14).

If, on the other hand, the Christian allows the Spirit of Christ (process *positiva*) to put to death and terminate the deeds of the "flesh" (cf. Gal. 5:19-21) and the body (process *negativa*), he will manifest the life and character of his Lord Jesus Christ, "the life of Jesus manifested in our mortal body" (II Cor. 4:11). It is important to note that it is "by the Spirit" that we "put to death" and terminatively disallow the expression of selfishly patterned physical and psychological desires.

As with the other processes used to describe the "process *negativa*" of dealing with sin in the Christian life, the "process of crucifixion" or death can be used legitimately to explain the process whereby our sinful patterns are disallowed and terminated. Those who use this metaphor of continuing death must be very cautious not to imply or allow that "the work of the cross" for the "death of self" is any performance action that results in sanctification.

Religionists have too often advocated a self-effort of an alleged "independent self" attempting to kill the selfishness of the "flesh." If the metaphor of inward death and crucifixion is used in Christian teaching, care must be taken to distinguish the once and for all historical death of Jesus Christ on the cross for redemption, and the initial crucifixion of the "old man" at regeneration, from the metaphor of "doing away with" sin patterns.

As worthy a theological thinker as Dietrich Bonhoeffer used the metaphor of an experiential cross, when he wrote: "The cross is laid on every Christian. . . . When Christ calls a man, He bids him come and die. . . . In fact every command of Jesus is a call to die, with all our affections and lusts."[10] Bonhoeffer was careful, however, not to lapse into any references to the cross being applied experientially in mystical, magical or idolatrous manners.

On the other hand, J. Sidlow Baxter referred to "the teaching . . . that sanctification comes through an inward crucifixion of the believer with Christ; a subjectively experienced dying with Him on the Cross," concluding, "I believe that this theory of death to sin by an inward crucifixion with Christ is error . . . It is not truly Scriptural; and those who presume to act upon it are exercising, not faith, but credulity."[11]

# The Resurrection-life of Jesus

Though the continued experience of the cross may be questioned, there can be no doubt of the Christian's experiential participation in the resurrection-life of Jesus. The life of the risen Lord Jesus is the ontological dynamic of all that is Christian.

Following the death of His friend Lazarus, Jesus declared to Lazarus' sister Martha, "I AM the resurrection and the life" (John 11:25). As the Son of God, Jesus had "life in Himself" (John 5:26), essentially and inherently. As the incarnate Son, capable of human mortality, Jesus was "obedient unto death, even death on a cross" (Phil. 2:8), and was "raised the third day, according to the scriptures" (I Cor. 15:4).

It was "impossible for the Sinless One to be held in death's power" (Acts 2:24), so Jesus was raised victorious over death and "declared the Son of God with power by the resurrection from the dead" (Rom. 1:4). By His resurrection Jesus became "the first born from the dead" (Rev. 1:5), "that He might be the first born among many brethren" (Rom. 8:29).

As the prototype of one who passed out of death into life, Jesus, the Victor Who had conquered death, made available to fallen and sinful man the opportunity to similarly "pass out of death into life" (John 5:24; I John 3:14) spiritually. The risen Lord became the "life-giving Spirit" (I Cor. 15:45), the "Spirit Who gives life" (John 6:63).

*The regenerative restoration of God's life in man
is predicated on the resurrection
of Jesus from the dead.*

Christians are "born again to a living hope through the resurrection of Jesus Christ from the dead" (I Peter 1:3). "When we were dead in trespasses and sins, God made us alive together with Christ" (Eph. 1:1,5). "We are dead to sin, but alive to God in Christ Jesus" (Rom. 6:11). "We have become united together with Him in the likeness of His resurrection" (Rom. 6:5), raised up with Christ (Eph. 2:6; Col. 2:12) to "walk in newness of life" (Rom. 6:4). "He who has the Son has life; he who does not have the Son of God does not have life" (I John 5:12).

"The Spirit of Him Who raised Jesus from the dead . . . gives life to our mortal bodies through His Spirit Who indwells us" (Rom. 8:11). Thus "reigning in life through Jesus Christ" (Rom. 5:17), Christians can experience the "abundant life" (John 10:10), the life of the risen Lord Jesus "manifested in our mortal bodies" (II Cor. 4:10,11) by the "power of His resurrection" (Phil. 3:10).

The objective of "having been raised up with Christ" is that we are to "keep seeking the things above" (Col. 3:1), i.e., allowing His living character to be expressed in our behavior, and considering ourselves dead to all that does not express His character (Col. 3:5).

Allowing the risen Lord Jesus to be our life (Col. 3:4) and living by His resurrection-life is the "process *positiva*" that facilitates the "process *negativa*" of terminating the selfish misrepresentative patterns of selfishness that remain in the desires of our soul.

Whereas, in the objective, historical redemptive actions of Jesus, physical death was necessitated for physical resurrection, and resurrection was predicated on such death, in the context of the subjective sanctification of the Christian the resurrection-life of Jesus effects and enacts all terminative endeavors that "put to death" the patterned propensities of selfishness.

The focus of the Christian should be on the resurrection-life of Jesus, and not on any death-efforts.

# 4

---

# Attempts to Deal with Sin
# by Self-effort

Throughout this study we have attempted to maintain the tensioned balance of the dialectic between the victory of Christ and His sufficiency as Lord in conjunction with the ongoing "saving life" of the Savior as He continues to deal with the sin-patterns of our lives as Christians.

We will now address what happens when the dialectic is not maintained, when the dynamic sufficiency of Christ's life is denied or minimized, and the issue of sin in the Christian's life is over-emphasized, particularly by self-determined attempts to deal with sin by self-effort. (cf. Left column of the chart – Addendum A)

Failing to understand that Christ alone can overcome sin, religionists concoct myriad self-actuated efforts to attempt to deal with sin and effect right behavior. The foundation of such performance-based effort to please and appease God is the fallacy of an alleged "independent self" capable of self-generated Christian ability and activity.

It would be impossible to enumerate all of the religious methods that have been proposed to negate one's misrepresentations of sinfulness and actuate one's own perfection. A brief list of some broad categories of religious self-effort will have to suffice.

## Activism

Many Christians are unaware that mottoes like, "Do your best and God will do the rest," and "God helps those who help themselves," are not in the Bible, and are in fact contrary to biblical instruction. God is not willing to serve as a "helper" who provides divine assistance for our self-improvement. He is not a "power booster" to enhance our self-empowerment.

The Creator God designed the human creature in such a way that it requires His presence and His action in man for man to function as He intended. God doesn't need any "help" in doing what only He can do in our lives, but that is not to deny that He respects our freedom of choice to be receptive in faith to His action.

Contemporary evangelical humanism seeks to make Christianity into a Christianized "self-help program." Constant encouragements to self-improvement are proposed. A popular theme of late was the question posed, "What Would Jesus Do?" (WWJD).

The premise behind the question was that a Christian should attempt to ascertain what Jesus would do in any given situation, and then "just do it" in the self-action of imitating Jesus.

The Christian life is not a self-generated "parroting" or "aping" of Jesus' example; it is not the imitation of Jesus, but the inhabitation of Jesus that allows for the manifestation of Jesus – "the life of Jesus manifested in our mortal bodies" (II Cor. 4:11).

Christians are often admonished to "*try* to rid themselves of sin," to "*try* to overcome the flesh," but that is a losing battle if there ever was one. The self-patterns will not be overcome by self-effort. On the other hand, we are told to "*try* to be better, *try* to be holy, *try* to be perfect." This is an "Avis Rent-a-Car" theology, with the motto, "*We try harder.*" God must find all of our trying very trying!

*The objective is not to strive to be "like Jesus" in order to arrive at "Christlikeness." The objective is to allow Jesus to live out His character and life in our behavior.*

The activism of religious disciplines has long been a means by which Christians have sought to thwart their sinfulness and perfect themselves. These include religious orders, vows, penances, indulgences, asceticism, monasticism, etc. Various methods of prayer, fasting, meditation, Bible reading and memorization, church attendance, and sacramental "means of grace" have also been advised. These disciplined activities can be advantageous in focusing our attention on the Lord, but only the living Lord Jesus can overcome our sin and energize divine character in our lives.

# Moralism

Many sincere Christians would define Christianity as an association of moral beings making moral choices to create a moral community. That might serve as a definition of a self-governing social unit, but it is woefully inadequate as a definition of Christianity.

Morality attempts to suppress the unacceptable (called "evil") and establish the acceptable (called "good") by humanly defined and self-determined standards of acceptability. God alone is good (cf. Mark 10:18; Luke 18:19), and the character of goodness can only be derived from Him (cf. III John 11).

Christianity is not morality. Christianity is not a believe-right, do-right religion based on behavioral conformity to acceptable codes of conduct. The Christian life is not an externally applied process of behavior modification based on "do this" and "don't do that," "thou shalt" and "thou shalt not."

Religion often emphasizes the responsibility of the adherent to overcome sin by the reformative self-disciplines of the renunciation of bad habits and resolution to live in accordance with the defined "good."

The words of Charles G. Finney are pointedly poignant:

> Many ministers and leading Christians give perfectly false instruction upon the subject of how to overcome sin. The directions that are generally given on this subject amount to this: "Take your sins in detail, resolve to abstain from them, and fight against them, if need be with prayer and fasting, until you have overcome. Set your will firmly against a relapse into sin, pray and struggle, and resolve that you will not fall, and persist in this until you form the habit of obedience and break up all your sinful habits." To be sure it is generally added: "In this conflict you must not depend on your own strength, but pray for the help of God." In a word, much of the teaching, both of the pulpit and the press, really amounts to this: Sanctification is by works, and not by faith.
>
> Now, what is resolved against in this religion of resolutions and effort to suppress sinful and form holy habits? Do we produce love by resolution? Do we eradicate selfishness by resolution? No, indeed. . . . To eradicate selfishness from the breast by resolution is an absurdity . . . All our battling with sin in the outward life, by the force of resolution, only ends in making us whited sepulchers. All our battling with desire by the force of resolution is of no avail . . . and will only end in delusion. . . . Away with this religion of resolution! It is a snare of death.[12]

A common moralistic technique for dealing with sinfulness is suppressionism – self-enacted attempts to push down, subdue, and restrain the selfish desires of the "flesh." Our selfishness patterns will never be kept down by self-will, which is the foundational premise of all selfishness. Suppression lapses into masochism and annihilationism in the common attempts to "die to self," and to "crucify self." It has been noted that self-crucifixion is impossible – though it might be possible to hammer the spike in one hand, there is no way to pin down the remaining hand, which remains free to facilitate selfishness.

The premise of self-generated right and moral behavior is rampant in the contemporary church. Hardly a sermon is preached that does not advocate commitment, dedication and consecration to better Christian living, to a "purpose driven life." This evangelical humanism that self-confidently promotes a self-righteousness by the self-action of Christian ability is a miscarriage, an abortion of God's grace.


# Legalism


Though law was superseded by grace in the new covenant of Jesus Christ, there is a constant tendency and temptation among Christians to revert to a law-based paradigm of behavior. "Christ is the end of the law for righteousness" (Rom. 10:4), because the external codification of behavioral rules and regulations has been superseded by "God's law written upon our hearts" (Jere. 31:33; Heb. 8:10; 10:16).

The indwelling dynamic of the life of Jesus Christ becomes the provision for manifesting divine character. Christ within the Christian is the inner "law of liberty"

(James 1:25; 2:12), allowing the Christian to live in the freedom of grace.

Despite the glorious freedom of Christian grace, there is a natural tendency to fall back into the false security of a legal system that tells us exactly what we should and should not do. Christian religion devises a "Christian law" that proscribes Christian commandments of acceptable behavior. This is the "Romans Seven Syndrome," the fallacy of constructing and submitting to law-strictures that are impossible to maintain.

Paul states the frustration of every Christian trying to keep the guidelines of "Christian law." "The good that I wish, I do not do; but I practice the very evil that I do not wish . . . Wretched man that I am!" (Rom. 7:19,24). Paul recognized, though, what every Christian is obliged to recognize: "If I am doing the very thing I do not wish, I am no longer the one doing it, but sin which dwells in me. I find then the principle that evil is present in me" (Rom. 7:20,21).

*Those sin-patterns of selfish action and reaction*
*in our fleshly desires are present in our soul,*
*but they do not constitute who we are,*
*our spiritual identity.*

Despite the behavioral conflict between the indwelling Spirit of Christ and the "flesh" patterns (Gal. 5:17), the Christian is not obliged to engage in the self-effort of self-righteousness in attempting to overcome the "indwelling sin" and live righteously.

"Thanks be to God" (Rom. 7:25), Paul exclaims, "there is therefore now no condemnation for those who are in Christ Jesus" (Rom. 8:1). The Christian need not experience any condemnation for the inability to live the Christian life by the fallacious "independent self" with its false premise of Christian ability by self-effort, for "the law of the Spirit of life in Christ Jesus has set you free from the law of sin and of death" (Rom. 8:2).

"What the law could not do, weak as it was through the self-effort of the flesh" (Rom. 8:3), the indwelling Spirit of Christ now accomplishes in the expression of the grace of God. Every Christian must come to this realization if they are to appreciate the victory that is theirs in Christ Jesus.

## Confessionalism

Failing to appreciate the sufficiency of God's grace, Christians who are attempting to overcome sin and live righteously by self-effort often develop an over-emphasized sin-consciousness. Oftentimes their attention is drawn to their sinfulness, rather than to the Savior. Their focus is on what they regard to be their "problem," rather than on the Person of Jesus Christ Who is their righteousness (I Cor. 1:30).

*Whenever our focus is on sinfulness,*

*we will be more inclined to sin.*

---

Our focus becomes a fixation and we are drawn like a moth to the fire. When our focus is on Jesus, we are drawn to Him and His sufficiency. "Fix your eyes on Jesus, the author and perfecter of faith" (Heb. 12:2).

The apostle John wrote, "If we confess our sins, He is faithful and just to forgive us our sins and to cleanse us from all unrighteousness" (I John 1:9). Christians are not without sin (I John 1:8), and need to agree and concur with God that their misrepresentative behaviors do not exhibit the character of God. Legitimate personal confession should not become an inordinate and obsessive confessionalism, however, that fails to experience the "cleansing from all unrighteousness" as Christ overcomes our sin-patterns with His righteous character.

Some religious communities encourage repetitive confessionalism by their adherents. Susceptible believers are encouraged to engage in introspective expeditions into their psyche to attempt to discover and dredge up sin, which only serves to verify their false identity of being a "sinner," rather than a regenerated "saint." The consequent feelings of worthlessness foster dependency on the priest or pastor.

When people rush to the altar each week, these "altar athletes" provide visible justification of the alleged effectiveness of the preacher's ministry. Some groups almost glorify sinfulness as members compete to see who can give the greatest "testimony" of their past sinfulness.

Such focus on sin and its confession also produces judgmentalism, for when one is always looking for sin in his own life, you can be sure he will be looking for sin in the lives of others also.

Undue preoccupation with sin in one's life is but an exercise of the "flesh." It is a self-concern based on the self-reliance that falsely believes that their self-generative "independent self" can overcome their sinfulness with self-effort, resulting in self-righteousness.

Only the Savior can overcome sin, and only the Righteous One can express His righteousness in our behavior.


## Defeatism

Eventually, Christians who are aware of their sinful propensities, and frustrated at their inability to conquer their shortcomings, begin to feel defeated. They may doubt their "salvation," whether they were really spiritually regenerated, since they have not been able to behave according to expected standards of Christian living. Others may revert to hypocrisy, willing to play-act as if they were successfully living the Christian life.

Some dismiss their defeat by falling back on human depravity and claiming, "I can't help but sin; I'm only human. I'm just a sinner saved by grace." Often quoting a verse that is only true of the unregenerate, they repeat, " 'The heart is deceitful above all things, and desperately wicked' (Jere. 17:9). What else can you expect of me other than failure?"

The more conscientious types who retain their expectations of self-perfection may beat themselves up in masochistic self-castigation for their failures. They berate themselves in self-condemnation and self-contempt, are critical of themselves in self-denigration and self-deprecation, and sometimes even engage in self-flagellation.

Since religion is codependent on the self-aspirations and failures of their followers, the continued sense of defeatism in their midst necessitated theological explanation and rationalization. This was accomplished in evangelical circles by devising a dual nature in the Christian individual and dual categories of Christians.

To explain the behavioral conflict in the Christian that often resulted in personal defeat, it was proposed that every Christian has "two natures." The old, fallen, depraved, selfish, sinful, Adamic, human nature of our unregenerate condition is alleged to exist alongside of a new, divine, Christ nature.

How can an individual have two inherent and essential constitutions or beings? Impossible! Since the real issue is life and death, it is impossible to have life and death simultaneously on the same plane. They are mutually exclusive.

The Greek word for "nature" is *phusis*, and

the New Testament is clear that when we were unregenerate we "were by nature (*phusis*) children of wrath" (Eph. 2:3). As Christians, we "have become partakers of the divine nature (*phusis*)" (II Peter 1:4). These natures do not exist simultaneously.

───────── ♥ ─────────

*The nature of man is the nature of the spiritual personage that indwells him – God or Satan.*

The "two natures" doctrine incorrectly translates the Greek word *sarx*, the word for "flesh," as "old nature." In so doing they facilitate a schizophrenic duality of identity in the Christian, a paranoid uncertainty of motivation, and antinomian excuses for Christian failure. The fallacious "two natures" theory allows a Christian to blame his sin on the alleged "old nature" that inhabits him.

Another explanation that excuses sin in Christians is the dividing of Christians into two categories. "Spiritual Christians" are those who allegedly are making the Christian life work by their active and moral endeavors to live in accordance with the Christian commandments. Those who have failed to overcome the "flesh" are designated as "carnal Christians," or "fleshly Christians."

To posit two types of Christian is entirely illegitimate. This separate "carnal Christian" category, popularized by the *Scofield Reference Bible*, Dallas

Theological Seminary, and the Campus Crusade for Christ organization, is a misinterpretation of the second and third chapters of Paul's first epistle to the Corinthians.

Paul identifies only two categories of people, the unregenerate and the regenerate, non-Christians and Christians, the "natural man" and the "spiritual man" (cf. I Cor. 2:14,15). There were some Christians in Corinth who were misrepresenting who they were in Christ by allowing fleshly patterns of selfishness to be expressed in their behavior, but this was not to be considered as inevitable or acceptable as a separate category of Christians in the Christian community.

The "carnal Christian" category has been used as a cop-out by many Christians to dismiss their sinful misrepresentation of Christ.

# 5

## Denial of the Need to Deal with Sin

Whereas the attempts to deal with sin by self-effort represent a failure to maintain the dialectic balance by diminishing or denying the sufficiency of Christ and focusing on independent endeavors to deal with the issue of sin, the opposite extreme denies the need to deal with sin by focusing on the completeness of the Christian's union with Christ and the total sufficiency of the life of Christ in the Christian. (cf. Right column of the chart – Addendum A).

The categories of activism, moralism, legalism, confessionalism, and defeatism that were utilized to explain the inordinate consciousness of sin are now reversed among those who eschew the preoccupation with sin, desiring to see "God only" in His victorious grace initiative to draw all men unto Himself. Their categories of emphasis include triumphalism, perfectionism, antinomianism, mysticism, and passivism.

# Triumphalism

To avoid any confusion with similar terminology, it is important that we define the type of triumphalism we are referring to. We are not addressing the religious triumphalism that regards Christian religion as superior to all other religions, or one denomination superior to other denominations. Neither are we speaking of social or political triumphalism that advocates the conquest of Christian ideology over all other worldly concepts. Eschatological triumphalism, the expected eventual triumph of the Kingdom of Christ at the end of time, is not our concern either.

The subject of our interest is the spiritual triumphalism that regards Christ's victory over sin to be efficacious to the extent that Christians no longer need to consider sin in their lives.

That Jesus Christ has triumphed over Satan (cf. Heb. 2:14; I John 3:8) and the forces of evil (cf. Col. 3:15) is not in dispute. Jesus exclaimed to His disciples, "I have overcome the world" (John 16:33). John likewise attests in his first epistle that Christians participate in Christ's victory: "Whoever is born of God overcomes the world" (I John 5:4). "God leads us in His triumph in Christ" (II Cor. 2:14), declares Paul. "We are more than conquerors through Him that loved us" (Rom. 8:37).

Spiritual triumphalism, however, asserts that Christ's redemptive and restorative action has drawn the Christian into spiritual union with Himself, "one spirit with Him" (I Cor. 6:17), to the extent that we have not just a relational oneness with Christ but an essential oneness with Christ. Affirming one's union identity with Christ, the Christian is encouraged to retain a fixed consciousness of "God only," without entertaining any consciousness of good and evil, or sin. They advocate having a "single eye," so that all you can see is God.

Absorbed into Christ in a monistic merging, the Christian is alleged to have totally replaced all sinfulness with His godliness, all humanity with His deity. In a contemporary form of Docetism, the Christian only "appears" to be human, but is really unified with the divine.

Everything the Christian does is said to be "Christ in action." "What I do is what He does. He acts as me." Even the misrepresentations of sin are merely "illusions," for they are really Jesus in action, and those who cannot see Him in the misrepresentation are failing to see "God only," unable to "see through" to God in action.

Let us be very straightforward here. Calling sin "Jesus" is blasphemy! Selfish and sinful expressions are not to be identified as "Jesus in your form," or "Jesus expressing His backside." This is totally unacceptable in any form of orthodox Christianity. It is a preposterous pretense whereby the diabolic deceiver masquerades behind an alleged spiritual triumphalism of oneness with the divine.

# Perfectionism

If "Spirit is the only reality," and sin is just an illusion, there need be no concern about dealing with sinfulness. "Sin is nothing," to be defined merely as the logical deprivation of perfection, and therefore denied in the Christian's life, and to be eliminated from Christian consciousness. The "inner" union with God's perfection is the only truth of significance, and the "outer" manifestations are irrelevant.

As justification for their perfectionistic perspective, they often quote II Corinthians 4:18, "We look not at the things which are seen, but at the things which are not seen; for the things which are seen are temporal, but things which are not seen are eternal." Taking the verse out of its context of comparing physical and glorified bodies, the spiritualist advocates advise Christians to "look above the line" by constant affirmation of the reality of their union-identity with Christ, while refusing to consider "below the line" actualities in the soul and body. In this manner they gloss over the entrenched selfishness in the behaviors patterns of their soul, refusing to let the Savior do His sanctifying work by His "saving life."

One way they excuse the avoidance of any consideration of their selfishness is by misusing Paul's statement, "The mind set on the flesh is death" (Rom. 8:6). Refusing to allow their conscious minds to dwell on the unreality of fleshliness, they repeat their mantras of essential unity with Christ and essential function "as Christ." The verse they use to justify their avoidance is taken out of context, for Paul was referring to the unregenerate mind set on selfish patterns of action and reaction as a "slave of sin." It is improper to use the verse as an excuse for the refusal to consider sin in one's life.

A particular enigma for their perfectionism is the passage in Romans 7 where Paul mentions the "sin that indwells me." How do they get around these words? They contend that Paul is posing a hypothetical fabrication, an illusory falsehood, a fictional lie that has no basis in fact, but is only a fallacious mental construct. What a convenient way to discount scripture that does not accord with your theories.

This kind of perfectionism goes far beyond the perfectionism of the holiness theologies. Though both reject the need for progressive sanctification in the Christian life, this union-perfectionism denies sin by refusing to accept its existence.

## Antinomianism

Seeking to avoid any trace of law-based religion with its legalistic demands, the Oneness teachers espouse a concept of grace that is not the active function of God in accord with His character, but is simply a reprieve from any expectations of obedience.

Focusing on their alleged freedom to live "as Christ," they often flaunt their liberty to the point that it becomes license and libertinism. Since they regard outer conduct of behavior to be irrelevant to their inner spirituality, they tolerate flagrant misrepresentations of the character of Christ in their midst. Setting themselves "above the law," they become a "law unto themselves."

## Mysticism

All genuine Christians participate in the "mystery of Christ Himself" (Col. 2:2), the "mystery which is Christ in you, the hope of glory" (Col. 1:27). This mystery was once concealed, but is now revealed in the new covenant participation of Christ's life.

Mysticism goes beyond the gospel mystery to aver an advanced spirituality that elevates the person beyond the earthly and worldly realm. They often claim to be "knowers" of enigmatic spiritual realities that ordinary people cannot know.

As contemporary Gnostics, they have an elitist attitude that boasts of "having arrived" at the pinnacle of "total-total truth." Claiming to be deified as co-creators, co-redeemers, and co-saviors with Christ, they are convinced they can "speak things into being" by a "word of faith." Their self-congratulatory spiritual pride is appalling.

## Passivism

In contrast to the activism of the other religious extreme, the spiritualists are content with passive irresponsibility. "Since all that you do, you do 'as Christ,' " they advise, "then, just 'be yourself.' "

"Trust that all you do is His doing. Trust yourself." This is countered by the proverbial wisdom, "He who trusts in his own heart is a fool" (Prov. 28:26).

# 6

## Personal Inability

We have observed the extremes that fail to maintain the dialectic balance, focusing on one track to the exclusion of the other. Those who refuse to address their sinfulness are unconcerned about and indifferent to the continuing saving work of Christ, and unless the convicting work of God's Spirit breaks into their heart they will be unlikely to respond with the humility that recognizes their need to allow Christ to function as Savior in their lives.

Those whose self-efforts at dealing with sin have led them to defeatism will, on the other hand, be more likely to admit their personal inability to conquer the selfishness of their "flesh," and will be more inclined to accept the all-sufficient grace of God whereby He overcomes sinfulness with His character of godliness.

Christians of the Western world in particular, because of their humanistic presuppositions of human ability to accomplish anything they set their minds to, often have a difficult time accepting personal inability. Thoroughly convinced that they are "independent selves" capable of self-governance, they are disinclined to admit that they are created as derivative and dependent creatures designed to be receptive in faith to God's action. But God has His ways of bringing us to the end of our self-confidence in our self-abilities to generate self-righteousness.

The habituated patterns of the "flesh" force many people to an admission of failure and helplessness, as their compulsive, obsessive and addictive propensities, their "besetting sins," repetitively conquer their flaunted will-power to overcome them.

The abundance of 12-step anonymity groups devoted to varying areas of life-dominating problems is evidence that many have been compelled to admit their inability to avoid succumbing to their selfish and sinful patterns of action and reaction. The self-help programs for reputed recovery from these patterns, even those with group accountability, seldom suffice to provide long-term resolution to the problems, often becoming an habituated crutch to assist in temporary suppression of the desires.

Combined with the frustration of repeated sinful expression of the desires of their "flesh," Christians who attempt to address their sinful weaknesses by the religious efforts of activism, moralism, legalism and confessionalism will also be forced into the defeatism of admitting that all the inculcations and incentives to overcome their selfish desires by religious techniques are doomed to failure.

The alleged Christian ability to live the Christian life by renunciation and resolution, by dedication and discipline, or by commitment and consecration is a bogus fabrication of an evangelical humanism that believes in the inherent power of an "independent self," capable of self-righteousness. The humanistic thesis of self-potential thrives on the modern religious calls for increased commitment and dedication, as well as the self-serving programs encouraging involvement and personal disciplines.

———— ♥ ————

*Even our fleshly failures and our religious defeats*
*serve God's purpose to expose our insufficiency*
*to be and do what God wants to be and do in our lives.*

As comedian Burt Rosenberg says, "You have to know what ain't, in order to know what IS. You have to know what doesn't work, in order to know Who does."

Paul explained, "Not that we are adequate in ourselves to consider anything as coming from ourselves, but our adequacy is of God" (II Cor. 3:5). Jesus told His disciples, "Apart from Me, you can do nothing" (John 15:5).

A.B. Simpson wrote,

The glory of the gospel is that it does not teach us to rise up to higher places, but shows our inability to do anything good of ourselves, and lays us at once in the grave in utter helplessness and nothingness, and then raises us up into new life, born entirely from above. The Christian life is not self-improving, but is wholly supernatural and Divine.[13]

The "Romans Seven Syndrome" mentioned earlier is the means that God often uses to cause the Christian to admit inability and defeat. When "law" becomes "Christian law," Christianized in commandments of expected performance and accepted as the legitimate basis of obedience, it serves its final purpose to expose our inability when we cry out, "The good that I would, I do not; and the evil that I would not, that I do" (Rom. 7:19).

Eventually, if we are sufficiently humiliated and honest, the worn-out Christian has to admit, "Lord, I can't! Leave it up to me and I'll blow it every time!" Such a cry of distress, the willingness to "give up" all self-attempts to live the Christian life, must be music to God's ears. We are then at the point of readiness to accept His ability, allowing the Christ-life to be lived out in, as, and through us.

The transition from Romans 7 to Romans 8 reveals "there is therefore now no condemnation for those who are in Christ Jesus" (Rom. 8:1) – no condemnation for admitting our inability to live the Christian life. "For the law of the Spirit of life in Christ Jesus has set you free from the law of sin and of death" (Rom. 8:2) – the dynamic of the Spirit of Christ has liberated us from the legalistic performance techniques of religion.

The Christian can now complete his exclamation, "I can't; only You can; I am willing to let You."

*"I can't"* – the cry of inability and defeat.

*"You can"* – the admission of divine ability.

*"I am willing to let You"* – the response of faith that is available to His ability, and receptive to His activity.

The first three steps of the common twelve-step recovery programs attempted to reproduce this sequence, but the replacement of the divine "You" with an impersonal "higher power" sacrificed the divine dynamic and opened the door for idolatry. Many Christians need to realize that the "you" who is able to solve their problems is not their counselor, their pastor, their spiritual mentor, their spouse or their friend, but only the divine "You" wherein is "the power of God unto salvation."

This sequence of statements sums up what the Bible refers to as "repentance," a word seldom heard in modern Christian teaching. Repentance is not simply the apology of saying, "I'm sorry," not the emotional chagrin of remorse, and not the masochism of self-chastisement.

The Greek word for "repentance" is *metanoia*, indicating "a change of mind that leads to a change of behavior." The change of mind is expressed by "I can't!" The change of action is facilitated by "He can, and I will let Him."

101

Repentance is a turning from self-effort to the acceptance of Christ's active expression of His life in our behavior. We must not, however, set out in self-effort to effect such repentance in our lives.

## "God will reveal it to you"

When Paul admitted to the Philippians that he "had not already become perfect" (Phil. 3:12) in behavioral manifestation, he went on to say, "If in anything you have a different attitude, God will reveal that to you" (Phil. 3:15).

———————— ♥ ————————

*God not only exposes our inability to deal with our fleshly desires by our own efforts, but He also reveals the particular areas of our selfishness that He wants to address and overcome.*

When He does reveal an area of selfishness, we are responsible to submit and do what is necessary to let Him deal with it. It may involve a "renewing of the mind" (Rom. 12:2; Eph. 4:23). It might involve refraining from or engaging in certain activities.

God works uniquely in each individual's life, for each Christian is a novel expression of the life and character of Jesus Christ. There is no formulized "how to" guide for living the Christian life. As previously noted, Christianity is not a morality structure of ethics demanding exacting conformity. It is important that Christians recognize the diversity and spontaneity of God's dealings and expressions in their own and in other Christians' lives. "Others May, You Cannot," wrote G. D. Watson (1845-1924), explaining that we are only responsible for responding to what God is doing in our own lives, without comparison to what He is doing in the lives of others.

Until God chooses to reveal what He wants to do in our lives, we should proceed with an inner peace that is not fretting about what we should or should not be doing. To engage in introspective expeditions of self-examination is often just another exercise in self-effort.

---------- ♥ ----------

*God is quite capable of directing our attention to what He wants to do in our lives.*

"He Who began a good work in you, will perfect it until the day of Christ Jesus" (Phil. 1:6). Proceed "in the clear" with your eyes straight ahead, focused on Him, and do not stop to "dig for worms." Enjoy every aspect of your life, unless, and until, God reveals that there is an issue of self-orientation that He wants to deal with.

This assumes, of course, that the Christian is being totally honest and available to the Lordship of Christ. But, if we are walking with the Lord, we should proceed with what we are doing and trust God to identify the issues of importance to Him. Too many Christians get waylaid in a self-concerned paranoia that keeps asking, "Is this me, or is this Jesus?" Since Jesus forms the basis of our new spiritual identity in Christ, we should be able to trust that Jesus is doing what He wants to do in us, as we remain open and available to Him.

The new covenant concept of "obedience" is not a law-based obedience that focuses on keeping rules and regulations, as the old covenant concept did. In the new covenant dynamic of the living Lord Jesus, the Greek word for "obedience" is *hupakouo*, which is to be translated "to listen under."

———— ♥ ————

*Christians are responsible to "listen under" the Lord to allow Him to reveal what He wants to do next in their lives.*

As Jesus said, "My sheep hear My voice" (John 10:1-16). When we perceive His direction by personal revelation, we can then respond in the "obedience of faith" (cf. Rom. 1:5; 16:26) that says, "Yes, Lord," and continues to be receptive to His activity, allowing Him to manifest His character in our behavior.

Only the Lord has the right to reveal sin and direct our Christian lives. Beware of any individual or religious group that attempts to usurp the Lord's prerogative to expose your selfishness or sin. If someone comes to you, saying, "The Lord has told me that you have this or that problem," disregard their intrusive input, explain that you have a personal relationship with the Lord that does not require intermediaries, and continue to listen to what Christ is revealing to you.

If a religious group seeks to engage in the collective catharsis of identifying sin in one another's lives, excuse yourself from participation in such. There are too many religious folk who seek to engage in the self-appointed position of attempting to "play Holy Spirit" in another's life.

On the other hand, be advised that when God does direct you to address an area of self-orientation or sinfulness in your life, it is only for you! Do not set out to apply to others what God has revealed to you. It is "personal revelation," not general revelation. Selfishly we are tempted to seek to involve as many people as possible in the crime. If we have been caught in the trespass of God's character, we think others should be exposed also, and sometimes set out on a crusade to "lay a guilt trip" on others for their similar attitudes or behavior.

Do not try to conduct God's business! Quietly let the Lord deal with whatever issues He brings to your attention, and allow Him to do the same in others. Remember, "love covers a multitude of sins" (I Peter 4:8).

## God's Grace Activity

The tragic misrepresentation of contemporary evangelicalism is their preoccupation with religious attempts to deal with sin and express righteousness by human self-effort. Their acceptance of the humanistic premise of an "independent self" that is allegedly capable of self-generating character in Christian behavior is a wholesale repudiation of God's grace.

When grace is mentioned in modern evangelical teaching it is often defined by the acrostic, "God's Redemption At Christ's Expense." Grace was indeed "realized through Jesus Christ" (John 1:17), and His incarnation and redemptive death serve to reveal God's grace, but grace must not be limited to the historical foundation of the Christian faith.

Going a step further, many recognize the personal experience of God's grace in spiritual regeneration, "for by grace you have been saved through faith" (Eph. 2:8). Someone has called this "the threshold factor"[15] of God's grace in the Christian life. But when Christ, the groom, carries another member of His bride, the church, across the threshold of initial regeneration, He does not "get them in the door" and then declare, "Now, straighten up and live like a Christian. Consider what I would do (WWJD) and live in accordance with My example." As Paul exclaims, "May it never be!"

Grace has a much broader and more dynamic meaning than is often projected in the teaching of the contemporary church.

106

*Grace is the totality of God's action
in total consistency with
His own Being and character.*

---

The Christian life cannot be lived by any human exertion, but only and entirely by God's grace. This forestalls any concept of an "infused grace" that acts as a divine assistance or a "power booster" to provide whatever the believer lacks to accomplish what God expects.

The activity of Jesus Christ our Lord and Savior, by the power of His Spirit, is the singular dynamic of Christianity. All manifestation of righteousness, holiness and godliness requires the presence and function of Jesus Christ, Whose very life and character supersedes, conquers and overcomes all unrighteousness.

This is how the prophet Ezekiel verbalized God's intents: "I will give you a new heart and put a new spirit within you; and I will remove the heart of stone from your flesh . . . I will put My Spirit within you and cause you to walk in My statutes, and you will be careful to observe My ordinances" (Ezek. 36:26,27).

Speaking through Zechariah, God promised, "Not by might nor by power, but by My Spirit, says the Lord of hosts" (Zech. 4:6). They foresaw the grace that was to be "realized in Jesus Christ" (John 1:17).

When the risen Lord Jesus Christ comes to live in us, we have the divine "treasure in earthen vessels, that the surpassing greatness of the power may be of God, and not of ourselves" (II Cor. 4:7) – there goes the humanistic thesis of self-potential! "God is at work in us, both to will and to work for His good pleasure" (Phil. 2:13). We are "strengthened with power through His Spirit in the inner man" (Eph. 3:16). The words of Jesus are clear: "Apart from Me, you can do nothing" (John 15:5).

Only the divine Savior can deal with the sinful and selfish patterns of our behavior. "By the Spirit you are putting to death the deeds of the body" (Rom. 8:13), Paul advised the Romans. "The Spirit sets its desires against the flesh" (Gal. 5:17) are the words he used to encourage the Galatians. Years later the apostle John wrote, "Greater is He Who is in you, than he who is in the world" (I John 4:4).

As we explained previously, the divine positive swallows up the sinful negatives. Since the "God Who is love" (I John 4:8,16) has come to live in Christians, "the love that controls us" (II Cor. 5:14) counters and overcomes the selfishness that is the opposite of all love.

God does not ask anything of us that He is not willing and prepared to do through us. He is ...
> the dynamic of His own demands,
> the content of His own commands,
> the expedient of His own expectations, and
> the means of His own mandates.

"This is the grace in which we stand" (Rom. 5:2) in Christ. "God is able to make all grace abound to you, that always having all sufficiency in everything, you may have an abundance for every good deed" (II Cor.

9:8). "He equips us in every good thing to do His will, working in us that which is pleasing in His sight, through Jesus Christ" (Heb. 13:21). We have "all power for the attaining of steadfastness and patience" (Col. 1:11), and "He will bring it to pass" (I Thess. 5:24).

That God does all that needs doing in our Christian lives is a truth that for some sounds "too good to be true." Worldly wisdom has cautioned us to beware of anything that sounds "too good to be true." Indeed, we should, but in this case the singularity of the good news of the gospel declaring that all the redemptive and restorative work of God is freely given by God's grace in Jesus Christ is the ultimate truth.

At the same time, be advised, for to accept God's grace will cost you everything. God's grace is not the "cheap grace" of a "free ride," but the "costly grace" that cost Jesus His life and will cost you yours as well.

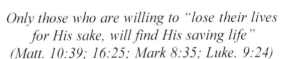

*Only those who are willing to "lose their lives*
*for His sake, will find His saving life"*
*(Matt. 10:39; 16:25; Mark 8:35; Luke. 9:24)*
*as their eternal gain.*

We often learn to appreciate the dynamic of God's grace in the Christian life only when we are brought to the "end of ourselves." When "our sin has found us out." When we have failed and are defeated. When we are brought to our knees by our own inability and weakness.

Paul was in the midst of such a situation when God advised him, "My grace is sufficient for you, for My power is perfected in weakness," and Paul responded, "Most gladly, therefore, I will rather boast about my weaknesses, that the power of Christ may dwell in me" (II Cor. 12:9).

We often have to experience what St. John of the Cross called the "dark night of the soul," wherein we cannot see our way through the dilemma we are dealing with and we despair even that God's grace will be sufficient.

---------- ♥ ----------

*We are "left in the dark"*
*to "walk by faith, and not by sight" (II Cor. 5:7)*
*until God's light shines forth*
*providing the life, energy, and action of His grace.*

Many Christians do not make it through the dark night of weakness wherein grace is revealed, for they are tempted to "take the easy way out" that bypasses the pain of what seems like estrangement. Thomas Merton explains how some exit the process for a way more exciting:

Paradoxically, then, though Christ Himself accomplishes the work of our sanctification, the more He does so the more it tends to cost us. The further we advance the more He tends to take away our own strength and deprives us of our human and natural resources, so that in the end we find ourselves in complete poverty and darkness. This is the situation that we find most terrible, and it is against that we rebel. For the strange, sanctifying mystery of Christ's death in us, we substitute the more familiar and comforting routine of our own activity: we abandon His will and take refuge in the more trivial, but more "satisfying" procedures which interest us and enable us to be interesting in the eyes of others. We think that in this way we can find peace, and make our lives fruitful; but we delude ourselves, and our activity turns out to be spiritually sterile . . . Insofar as we rely on our own anxious efforts, we are of this world.[16]

Divine grace does indeed run counter to all enlightenment understanding and humanistic reasoning. It makes no sense to our American work ethic, our pragmatic concerns for productivity, and our capitalistic premise that "you get what you pay for." The mentality of the world will always regard grace as an escapist pattern of indolent inertia and sloth for those who disdain work and prefer to be "on the dole" in God's kingdom.

The contemporary religion of "evangelical humanism" has the same point of view, suspicious that the gospel of grace leads only to passivism and acquiescence that will never serve to build an active church organization. Only the Christian who has submitted himself to God's grace will see it for what it is – the divine dynamic of Christ's life that alone can overcome sin and manifest God's character.

# Our Response of Faith

Contrary to the charge that grace fosters passivism and inaction, the human individual is always responsible to function as a contingent, choosing creature who derives character and action from a spirit source.

The responsibility of man is best understood as his response-ability to God, His Creator. This response-ability of faith will never produce passivism if we correctly understand that faith is "our receptivity to His activity." Inherent in such a definition is the active expression of God's grace.

Faith, thus defined, allows us to understand the statements of James when he wrote that "faith without works is dead" (James 2:17,26) and "faith without works is useless" (James 2:20).

———————— ♥ ————————

*Faith (our receptivity of His activity)*
*without works (the outworking of God's grace activity)*
*is dead, useless, and non-existent*
*(by the privation of the activity inherent in the terms).*

When faith responds in receptivity to God's grace activity, passivism is out of the question because God is not a passive God, but always acts in accord with His character, His Being in action.

In his commentary on Paul's epistle to the Romans, Martin Luther reacts to religious misconceptions of faith.

> They conjure up an idea which they call "belief," which they treat as genuine faith. It is but a fabrication, an idea without a corresponding experience in the depths of the heart. It is ineffective and not followed by a better kind of life. Faith puts the old Adam to death and makes us quite different men in heart, in mind, and in all our powers. A man not active in this way is a man without faith.[16]

When the Christian's receptivity of faith avails itself to God's activity of grace, there will be an inevitable counteraction against all that is contrary to God's character.

God always acts in accordance with His character and in order to express His character within His creation unto His own glory. Sin falls short of the glory of God (cf. Rom. 3:23), for sin is any expression of character that is not God's character. Sin is not defined by certain unacceptable actions, but by anything less than the character of God.

When the Christian fails to respond in faithful receptivity to God's active expression of His character, then the only alternative to God's action will be a sinful expression of evil character, derived from a source other than God. Despite how religious and pious the action might appear externally, "whatever is not of faith is sin" (Rom. 14:23), and "the one who sins derives what he does from the devil" (I John 3:8).

Receptivity of God's character and activity in faith, both initially and continuously, will exclude sin in the Christian's life. Commenting on the incompatibility of faith and sin, J. Gresham Machen wrote,

> Faith involves a change of the whole nature of man; it involves a new hatred of sin and a new hunger and thirst after righteousness. It is inconceivable that one could accept the gift which Christ offers, and still go on contentedly in sin. For the very thing which Christ offers us is salvation from sin – not only salvation from the guilt of sin, but also salvation from the power of sin.[18]

The holy character of God expressed in human behavior for the purpose of God's glory is the objective of all Christian faith. This process of sanctification – of receptivity to the expression of God's holy character by the active manifestation of the "Holy One" (Acts 2:27; 3:12; 13:35), Jesus Christ, dwelling in the Christian – is what constitutes Christianity. J.C. Ryle makes this quite clear in his treatise on "Holiness."

> Sanctification is the invariable result of vital union with Christ. The branch which bears no fruit is no living branch of the vine. The union with Christ which produces no effect on heart and life is a mere formal union, which is worthless before God. The faith which has not a sanctifying influence on the character is no better than the faith of devils. It is a "dead faith, because it is alone." In short, where there is no sanctification of life, there is no real faith in Christ.[19]

By faith the Christian opens himself up to God's activity in Jesus Christ. We give up our alleged right to control our own lives by submitting to the loving control of the Lordship of Jesus Christ. From the brokenness of our admitted powerlessness, we cry, "Whatever You want, Lord."

We have all made that concession when confronted with a crisis, or when faced with a particularly tough trial, but receptive faith must become a continuity in our lives. Not just when we are facing an emergency, a surgery, a divorce, job loss, bankruptcy, incarceration, etc., but constantly, moment by moment, day in and day out, an abandoned availability to whatever the Lord Jesus Christ wants to be and do in our lives.

When faith is thus understood as submission and surrender to God and His desires, we cannot conceive of faith as an instrumental means to achieve a particular end. We do not respond in faith in order to become mature or "spiritual." Faith is not to be regarded as a means to become a spiritual "knower" or a spiritual "father."

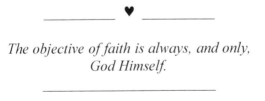

*The objective of faith is always, and only, God Himself.*

Not that we become God, but that we are available to whatever He wants to do.

A constant prayer of faith can be verbalized throughout the day in the simple affirmation, "Yes, Lord!" "Yes, Lord, I want Your character to be

expressed in this situation." "Yes, Lord, show me the
next opportunity to let the Christ-life be manifested"
(cf. II Cor. 4:11). "Yes, Lord, You will not allow me to
be tempted beyond what I am able" (I Cor. 10:13).
"Yes, Lord, You will keep me from stumbling" (Jude
24). "Yes, Lord, You will cause me to stand" (Rom.
14:4).

If "Yes, Lord" were the extent of one's prayer
vocabulary, that individual could be walking in the
"obedience of faith" (Rom. 1:5; 16:26) and "praying
without ceasing" (I Thess. 5:17).

The Christian response of faith is beautifully
expressed in the words of the hymn written by Adelaide
A. Pollard:

> Have Thine own way, Lord!
> Have Thine own way!
> Thou art the Potter;
> I am the clay.
> Mould me and make me,
> After Thy will,
> While I am waiting,
> Yielded and still.

> Have Thine own way, Lord!
> Have Thine own way!
> Hold o'er my being
> Absolute sway!
> Fill with Thy Spirit
> Till all shall see
> Christ only, always,
> Living in me!

# Conclusion

---

The superficiality of contemporary acculturated ecclesiasticism is truly disturbing. Their response to the message of "Christ at work in you" is often, "Don't be an extremist. Don't be a fanatic. Don't be a puritanical pietist. Don't be a mystical spiritualist." They would prefer that church members simply "go through the motions" of conforming to the established program, willing to be committed and involved by attending the services, tithing their income, and espousing a particular social agenda. The well-oiled ecclesiastical machine thus remains statistically viable, though spiritually bankrupt.

While we have no illusion of reforming the institutional church, we are fully convinced that many Christian individuals who comprise the Body of Christ are desirous of the fullness of Christ's life. It is you for whom this book has been written, and may God use it to speak to your heart.

Perhaps you have been an active church member for many years and never realized that "Christ is your life" (Col. 3:4), that He jealously desires to function as

Lord and Savior in every detail of your life. "Now may the God of peace Himself sanctify you entirely; and may your spirit and soul and body be preserved complete" (I Thess. 5:23) as Christ becomes "all in all" of your life.

Some of you who read this book have seldom, if ever, taken the time to slow down and listen to God in Christian obedience. So busy living under the premise of an "independent self" who is obliged to please and appease God, you may never have considered how the living Lord Jesus Christ wants to manifest His "saving life" to overcome your sin-patterns of habituated selfishness. As you "listen under" God, may you understand the grace wherein Paul exclaimed, "I can do all things through Christ Who strengthens me" (Phil. 4:13).

On the other hand, some of you have participated in long introspective expeditions to uncover your sinfulness. You may have been overwhelmed with the guilt of being caught in your trespasses, and felt the hot coals of self-condemnation for your inability to suppress your selfishness and gain victory over your weaknesses. There is no longer any need to labor under the strictures of a "do-right religion." You can experience the freedom of Christ's work in you, remembering that Jesus said, "Apart from Me, you can do nothing" (John 15:5).

Some of you who read these pages may have trafficked on God's grace. In spiritual pride you may have claimed spiritual "union with Christ" and refused to consider the residual sin-patterns in your soul. Do not resist the work of Christ as Savior in your life, whereby

He continues "to save His people from their sins" (Matt. 1:21).

Whatever our past Christian experiences have been, we all have the opportunity to yield to Christ's work in us as Lord and Savior. By allowing Him to manifest His character of godliness, and thus overcome our sinfulness, "the fruit of the Spirit which is love, joy, peace, patience, kindness, goodness, faithfulness, gentleness, and godly control of the self" (Gal. 5:22,23) will be the evidence of "Christ at work in us."

# Endnotes

1   Bonhoeffer, Dietrich, *The Cost of Discipleship*.
    New York: Macmillan Publishing Co. 1963. pg 47.
2   Pink, A.W., *Studies in the Scriptures*. Edinburgh:
    Banner of Truth Trust. Dec 1937. pg 21.
3   Grubb, Norman P., *The Deep Things of God*.
    Fort Washington: Christian Literature Crusade.
    1974. pg 25.
4   Tozer, A.W., *I Call It Heresy*. Harrisburg, PA:
    Christian Publications. 1974. pg 16.
5   Tozer, A.W., *Ibid.*, pg 18.
6   Merton, Thomas, *Life and Holiness*. New York:
    Image Books, Doubleday. 1996. pg 12.
7   Merton, Thomas, *Ibid.*, pg 57.
8   Merton, Thomas, *Ibid.*, pg 79.
9   Grubb, Norman P., *The Law of Faith*. Fort
    Washington: Christian Literature Crusade. 1972.
    pg 31.
10  Bonhoeffer, Dietrich, *Ibid.*, pg. 99.
11  Baxter, J. Sidlow, *Our High Calling*. Grand
    Rapids: Zondervan Publishing House. 1967.
    pg 163.
12  Finney, Charles G., "How to Overcome Sin." *The
    Independent of New York*. New York: January 1,
    1874. Later published as chapter 10 in *Power
    From on High*. 1944.

13  Simpson, A.B., *The Christ Life and the Self Life*. Camp Hill: Christian Publications, Inc. n.d. pg 109.

14  Fowler, James A., *Christ in us. Christ as us. Christ through us*. Fallbrook; CA: C.I.Y. Publishing. 2001.

15  Smith, Joe Carson, article entitled "The Reality of Grace" in *Christian Standard*. Cincinnati: Standard Publishing. December 9, 1979. pgs 6-7.

16  Merton, Thomas, *Ibid.*, pg 117.

17  Luther, Martin, *Preface to Romans*. Grand Rapids: Kregel Publications. 1977. pg xvii.

18  Machen, J. Gresham, *What is Faith?* Grand Rapids: Wm. B. Eerdmans Publishing Co. 1946. pg 204.

19  Ryle, J.D., *Holiness*. Wilmington: Associated Publishers and Authors, Inc. n.d. pg 11.

20  Pollard, Adelaide A., "Have Thine Own Way Lord!" Copyright 1907 by G.C. Stebbins. Assigned to Hope Publishing Co.

Made in the USA
Middletown, DE
07 August 2016